About the Author

Martin burns down every bridge and anything good he builds in his life. The only thing he is good at is being a parent to his three kids.

This is Not a Suicide Letter

Martin Douglas

This is Not a Suicide Letter

Olympia Publishers
London

www.olympiapublishers.com

OLYMPIA PAPERBACK EDITION

Copyright © Martin Douglas 2024

The right of Martin Douglas to be identified as author of
this work has been asserted in accordance with sections 77 and 78 of
the Copyright, Designs and Patents Act 1988.

A CIP catalogue record for this title is
available from the British Library.

ISBN: 978-1-80074-857-6

First Published in 2024

Olympia Publishers
Tallis House
2 Tallis Street
London
EC4Y 0AB

Printed in Great Britain

Dedication

For Jaz, my guardian angel.

Acknowledgements

To my kids, if you ever read this, don't be like Dad. I love you.

This Is Not a Suicide Letter

Having a mental illness has become a fad these days. Every man and their dog has one. A must-have accessory to go with their designer clothes and Instagram filters. People proudly declare their ailments on social media to show how brave they are about opening up. Depression is the new craze, and unless it's 'Facebook official', then it doesn't exist. True sufferers suffer in silence. Their illness is hidden away, and any ailments that do show are covered for, like an abusive lover. I am alone in a room full of people but simultaneously stalked by my tormentor.

Where is there to turn to when your own consciousness is your enemy? A ghost in the daylight. One slip in concentration and your train of thought about what to buy your son for his birthday can derail into how he would be better off without you and how good you would look swinging from a tree you just glanced at out of the window. You don't see posts like this shared and liked and have the cure confirmed as a yoga regime or fucking cold water therapy.

How do I know that I have never been truly happy? It's because I don't want it. The thought of being happy makes me sick. I'm happy wallowing in my misery, cocooned in hate and rebelling from any help I am offered. My would-be saviours are painted as villains that give me purpose to fight against them. I kick back at the world, but the world kicks back a lot fucking harder. If I knew what happiness was, I would grab it with both hands. Run towards it screaming incoherent apologies. Take it, never let it go and never look back into the howling abyss that I once made my home.

When injecting good cocaine, you can taste it. It is a peculiar sensation that can easily be missed with the whooshing head rush that accompanies it. Senses flare and become acutely more aware, heart rate skyrockets, libido increases and eyesight narrows to a pinprick. Awareness of your surroundings shrinks, but the focus of your attention is shown in that much better clarity. Adrenaline surges, and pleasure receptors are swamped. You can feel colours and taste the fucking rainbow. You can see how this feeling is a hard thing to give up, especially when you are sad and scared to begin with.

Overdosing on shooting coke is not as unpleasant as people would make you believe. There is an onset of tremors, which feels like a satisfying scratch of an itch you never knew you had. The shakes make it a mission to put the cap over the needle you have just drawn out of your vein, and you get a rush of pride when it is sheathed. Saliva fills your mouth, like Pavlov's dog, then you fall into a deep sleep. Pity, this is the coke trying to kill you.

I miss both feelings like a part of my soul, a soul that I sold long ago to buy drugs. The high took away the voices in my head, then the creeping low of overdose wrapped me in a blanket as I knew my pain was coming to an end.

For as long as I can remember, I have been hell-bent on self-destruction. Forming scars and burning bridges on my quest to find something elusive that was missing in my life. I became convinced, it was my own death, and I took solace in this. Took pride in my arrogant death wish, oblivious to the collateral damage it caused to those who loved me.

I started hearing voices about two months before the birth of

12

my second son and seven months before my overdose.

My head has always been a dark place to live. The official prognosis is bipolar and borderline personality disorder. Lovely titles. I just assumed I was more susceptible to depression and far more susceptible to going off the rails. I have always felt a hole inside me, a void I am unable to fill, no matter what I do. Every time things are going good in my life, I am compelled to push the self-destruct button and I have worn it down to a nub.

The voices started as a barely audible whisper, a constant background noise to my already fragile mind. I would occasionally get full visual hallucinations accompanying the voices. Knee-high fog with tendrils that would coalesce into grasping hands. These episodes never really scared me in the beginning, but I knew not to listen closely to the whispers. They were beckoning me, asking me to join them. My psychiatrist would later tell me that these hallucinations can be caused by excessive cocaine abuse. This was not the case with me, or so I tell myself. The voices came first, and I used drugs as a crutch to escape them. Drugs were a symptom of my madness, not the cause.

As the voices became more insistent and sinister, I used drugs as a safety blanket. They turned down the volume of the world inside and out of my head.

But whispers became shouts, and the shouts became screams. Every night, when my family went to sleep, the house would become quiet, and I had nothing to focus my attention on other than the voices, my insistent companions. I became convinced I had to die. It was preordained. I craved it. The voices became my friends, and I longed to join them.

Each line I took would make it more appealing. Pregabalin and coke filled me up, and madness was carrying me away.

(Pregabalin, or Goblin's, as I call them, is a prescription pill I was prescribed to help my anxiety and stop seizures. If a high enough dose is taken, its like a warm cuddle, similar to heroin I've been told. I was addicted within weeks and taking ten times the normal dose, topping up my prescription by buying extra online.)

During the days and weeks over the Christmas holidays, my head was a cacophony of conflicting voices.

I was awake for seventy-two hours the day my second son was born. This was due to crippling anxiety that the birth would go wrong. Holding my son for the first time nearly burst my heart. My kids are the best things in my life, my greatest achievement and the only things I am proud of. I love them endlessly, but the greatest gift they give me is silence. When I am with them, just silence. Blessed silence in my head. I could live there forever.

The voices are patient though and wait for me. As soon as my guard is down or I am away from my kids, the demons claw their way back in. Or out. During this time, hiding my addictions became a full-time occupation. I lied endlessly, manipulated my friends and family and wheeled and dealed narcotics to fund my own habit. Sometimes, in the darkest moments of my addiction, I would ask myself, why can't they catch me? How do they still not know? When all my illicit addictions came to light, I was so relieved. But then I found a new addiction. Everyone telling me what I could not do made me determined to do it. Duping people became my new occupation. Still managing to hide being a junkie even when my loved ones knew what to look out for. I am a horrible person.

My wayward death style was taking its toll on my nose. A nose that I have abused over the years. My life story could have been called *Me and My Nose*. It has been broken several times, mostly because I am always talking when I should be listening. The tip has been bitten off during a fight, and I have snorted every drug I could get my hands on. I needed to give my nose a rest from the cocaine, but the voices were unrelenting. I needed a new method of delivery.

There is more than one way to skin a cat, so crack was my answer. I was always curious about it, so I decided to kill the fucking cat and cook the coke up myself. I fell in love with the whole ritual of cooking. Burning the spoon and watching the coke and bicarb coalesce into crack. Watching the oil start to float on the water is magical; I think I liked it more than smoking the rock.

The transition from pipe to needle was as natural as growing old to me. Again, I fell in love with the ritual. Finding a vein then the initial pull of blood is like the deep breath before the plunge. The anticipation that builds only stands to heighten the cocaine rush. When you end the anticipation and send the coke rushing through your blood stream, it's like your ears pop with pressure, your head goes fuzzy and all your senses are turned up to eleven. Unless you have been there, you won't understand the struggle of intense paranoia you get when you are trying to secretly draw up a shot. Your whole world slows down, and you forget to breathe so much you only notice it when you hear your heartbeat slow.

But it swept the voices away like a flood. I was in love and addicted instantly. Injecting cocaine wasn't my drug of choice, it was my drug of no choice.

Thus, was the descent into my madness and the game played for my soul.

The day I died was just like any other. In the morning, I sat looking out for the postie like a wee boy waiting for Santa, as I was expecting a half q of uncut coke that I ordered online. When I opened the package and saw the lump of coke, I was grinning like the Cheshire Cat. I numbed myself the rest of the day with Goblin's and hid my psychosis from my family. I could still change nappies, play *Minecraft* with my older son and fuck my wife, but once they all went to sleep, the demons crawled out of the walls and out of my head.

The downstairs bathroom was like my security blanket, panic room and drug den all rolled into one. I went in, took my time and enjoyed following the recipe to cook up a gram of crack. At about two in the morning, the crack was gone, and I was too anxious and jittery to cook up more, so I moved on to the needle. I have never weighed the Ching before I mix it in water. I have always eyeballed it, but this was not a good idea, considering my eyeballs were popping out my skull.

The coke was so pure that it dissolved straight away, leaving no residue, but I still used a part of a cotton bud as a filter and drew up a full 1 ml syringe. As soon as I finished pushing the plunger, I knew I was in trouble. My arms started shaking first, and I didn't have time to pull the needle out before a full body intense convulsion threw me off my sitting position on the toilet. I smacked the bridge of my nose on the sink (another broken nose) and collapsed onto the floor. Lights out, goodnight, bon voyage.

Stars

I came to lying on my back in about an inch of cold water, and all I could see was stars. I felt brand new. Like a reset button had been pressed in my body. It is the feeling you get after a seizure. Your body shakes the evil out of you, like a dog shaking his coat to get the water off after a swim. A sea of infinite stars above and reflected in the water below surrounded me.

There was a man standing over me. He was middle-aged, handsome with a shaved head and was smiling at me like he knew all the secrets of the world. He was wearing faded denim jeans and a black long-sleeved jumper with crimson slashes on both shoulders. He extended a hand to help me up and spoke.

"Hey, Marty, my name is Rand. Made a cunt of it here, ain't you."

Despite his charming tone and smile, one look at his eyes and all you could see was trouble. The intensity of them set you on edge. When I grabbed his hand, his skin felt reptilian and seemed to shift under my grip. His hold on my hand was like a vice and so cold I went numb up to my elbow. He pulled me up with a jolt, and I first fully took in my surroundings. The inch of water I was lying in stretched to the horizon in every direction. The stars above and reflected below were the only source of light. The milky way, closer and brighter than I had ever seen it before, stretched in an arc above like a giant serpent drifting lazily through the sky.

"Where am I?"

"Look down," he said, still grinning like a madman. The grin of Christian Bale as Patrick Bateman.

About ten feet below the surface, I could see my bathroom, where I had passed out. I could see myself and my wife frozen in time. I was wearing nothing but my blue shorts, and the top half of my body was covered in blood. My back was arched like I was in the middle of a massive convulsion, and I still had the needle hanging out of my left arm. (I was wearing the same blue shorts right now, but I was blood and syringe free.) I was as skinny as I have ever been due to months of drug abuse. Each rib on display was a harsh underline of my habits.

My gorgeous wife looked nearly as pale as I did. Normally, she is a short blonde with defined features and a button nose. But now her hair was all tangled, her face was contorted in terror, and she looked to be screaming down the phone held to her ear.

"Am I dead?" I whispered, not really having registered what was going on yet.

"It has not been decided," said another voice over my shoulder. I turned around to see a short man dressed in black jeans and a baby-blue shirt. The most striking thing about him was that his face was completely transparent. All you could see through it were the stars behind him. Featureless, with a shimmering outline of a head. The stars seen through his face also seemed to shine brighter and pulse with the fluctuations of his voice. He seemed a stranger and a lifelong friend to me all at once. Conflicting emotions were made stronger when I noticed the Glaswegian accent he spoke with.

"Look, what you have become, Marty." Softly spoken and genuine, as if the yin to Rand's yang. Good cop, bad cop, but both still fucking pigs in my eyes.

"Right, what the fuck is going on, and who are you?" My initial fear was replaced by my usual knee-jerk reaction of anger whenever my behaviour is challenged, or I find myself in a

18

situation I am not in control of.

"You know who I am, Marty, or you are still too blinded by drugs to notice, for now call me Bill. You are in your own personal purgatory. Forged by your misdeeds. You have not chosen if you want to live or if you have any soul that you want to redeem. This leads on to the question of what will become of you if you die." His voice swimming with tones of concern and melancholy.

"We are going to go back to pivotal moments in your life. You will see all your fuck ups, all your sins and all your failings. You will see the folly made of your life. The first steps on the path to the lovely scene below." Rand smiled. It wasn't so much a smile as a crack in his face. A chasm of evil.

"You have had a death wish for a long time. You have turned into a black hole, sucking in everything around you and radiating misery."

"This is important," Bill said, putting a hand on my shoulder. Looking into his face gave me a sense of vertigo. Like I could fall into the stars within his face. "You need to realise what went wrong in your life so you can piece together what you have left. If not, you will get the death you have craved, and what comes after won't be pleasant."

My head was spinning, and I had to fight my initial gut reaction to rebel. I fought my anger and swallowed the insults and demands.

"So, this is like a fucking *Christmas Carol* for junkies," was as pleasant as I could reply.

Rand burst out laughing. "I suppose you could call it that. Your everlasting soul is on the line, after all." He placed his hand on my chest, gave a slight shove, and I went flying backwards through time.

Kidnapped on Halloween

It's 2004, and I am a fresh-faced nineteen-year-old. This is before my several broken noses and facial scars. They say that only teenagers and junkies have real six-packs, and I am a bit of both, so needless to say I would have to run around in the shower to get wet. I have short brown hair, a prominent nose (a target, it would seem), a defined jaw line and women's eye-lashes. I have been called a pretty boy, although this may be to do with occasionally wearing eyeliner. I have a look about me that lets me get away with murder.

I am drinking in my bedroom in my parents' house with Grant. Grant is tall and handsome in an ugly sort of way, with a slow wit, a fast temper and one hundred per cent full of shite. Always bigging himself up. If you have been to Tenerife, then he has been to Elevenerife. If he ever met Neil Armstrong, he would be telling him that he has been to Mars.

My parents have always had an open-door policy with my friends, but I think it's more so they can keep an eye on me other than their altruistic nature. I remember when I was thirteen or fourteen, back in the time before mobile phones, I was speaking to a girl on the house phone in my room. I was telling her how I would use a condom when we had sex, so there would be no mini-me's running about. All of a sudden, my mum butts in and shouts, "You stay away from my son." She was eavesdropping from the phone downstairs, and I was grounded for two weeks. Punished for sex I had never had, it was a prelude of what is to follow.

We are both dressed as the guys from the 118 adverts for Halloween. For the philistines among you, the 118 adverts were for a sort of phone book where you would phone a switchboard and they would give you any number you needed, and it ran in the early noughties. It was two white guys with afros and handlebar moustaches dressed only in white vests and red shorts who would run into random shops and do push ups and squats.

I chose the costume, as I fucking love Halloween. I love it more as an adult that I did as a kid, I think just because I can pretend to be someone else for the night. Even at nineteen, the hole had appeared inside me, and I never felt comfortable in my own skin. We were downing glasses of vodka and Irn-Bru (still my favourite drink to this day, although I drink normal measures now, not the half-vodka half-mixer glasses I used to pour) and playing cards. The card game was irrelevant: it only served to give forfeits to your opponent so they would get drunk quicker. It was customary among my group of friends to finish a 70 cl bottle of vodka each before we even set foot in a pub. Customary among most Scottish youths, I imagine. Once suitably lubricated, we jump into a taxi to head to the com.

The commercial hotel and I have had a love – hate relationship over the years. It was the only pub to go to for young people on a Friday and Saturday night in our shitty one-horse town. Alness is a drug-ridden sore, festering with poverty set in the idyllic Scottish Highlands. A blemish on the face of a natural beauty. It is on the coast of a deep-water port that once served military warships but now caters to most of the North Sea's oil rigs. This means a convergence of all the workers needed to keep this dying industry alive. They don't call them roughnecks for nothing.

21

Alness actually has a nice high street with respectable surrounding housing schemes. Unfortunately, it is caught in a pincer by Westford and Milnafua. Run-down council estates so full of drugs that it was easier for me when I was underage to buy eccies and speed than it was to buy alcohol. Each weekend, the residents of both council estates would descend inward like ants swarming an invader to their nest, trying to purge the middle-class high street from their circle of a lower-class parody.

Back to the com. I have had it closed early once by the police, because I got a kicking in the smoking area then wandered back into the bar trailing blood everywhere. I have fucked girls in the toilets, and I have been barred more times than I can count. The first was the night of my eighteenth birthday, which was so long ago, you could still smoke in the pubs. Near the end of the night, a particularly annoying waitress was collecting the full ashtray from our table, and I pretended to have an elaborate sneeze into it, covering us and the rest of the table in fag ash. We looked like miners after a hard day's graft.

We jogged out of the taxi and into the lounge and immediately started doing press ups at the bar, which to my inebriated mind was to roars of laughter and thunderous applause. In reality, it was a few snickers from the drunk regulars.

"Fucking hell, I'm pishing sweat," Grant said with heavy breath.

No wonder – he had already necked three of our ten eccies a half hour previous. He had pupils like dinner plates and couldn't stand still. I ordered us both a drink and asked if he was coming for a seat.

"Na, Marty, I can't," he twitched as he headed for the dance floor and proceeded to do "Big Fish Little Fish Cardboard Box" and "Feed the Pigeons".

22

I took a seat at the back of the lounge next to Steve (or Moley, or Sir Molealot, king of Sciroccos. He was called this due to a hardly noticeable mole he had on his chin and slightly flaky arms), who was dressed as Batman. One thing about my group of friends (or Scottish people in general) that I love is that we took the piss out of each other relentlessly. Any insecurity or mistake in life was pounced upon and used as ammo. My friend once took what he thought was a seductive topless pic to send to a girl in return for a tit pic. He showed it to our group, and it was commented on that he looked like a foetus. The nickname stuck, and nearly twenty years later, I managed to find the photo on an old laptop, had it blown up and presented to him as a wedding present.

Steve was sitting next to my girlfriend, Rebbecca. We don't usually mix on a night out, as to say we had a dysfunctional relationship would be putting it lightly. I found out she cheated on me after we were going out for a year, and looking back, I think that set the tone for how I would handle all my relationships. My mindset was, I'm going to cheat on them as much as I can so that no matter what they do to me, I will always have done worse. This is not me absolving myself of any blame; I can just see now it was the catalyst for my years of infidelity.

"Do you know Frank was at the door looking for you earlier? He was demanding to get in, and they had to threaten to call the police to get him to leave," Rebbecca said.

"Honestly? Fuck sake," I said despondently.

Frank is a six-foot-three nutter, who is built like a brick shithouse. The last time he had been looking for me, he and his brother gave me a kicking in a nightclub toilet then tried to flush my head down the pan. Only my vice-like grip on the cubicle doors and the arrival of a bouncer saved me that humiliation. I thought the head-flushing thing was only something bullies did in shitty cartoons. Then they had the cheek to approach me in a taxi rank later that night and ask to share a lift home.

I had no idea why he was looking for me, and I should have given more weight to the fact, but I looked over and saw Grant grinding on what looked like the Gruffalo. Grant dancing with her reminded me of someone trying to move a fridge. I pushed Frank and the ominous tones of his search for me to the back of my mind.

The night progressed as normal. I got drunker and took my eccies to level out, with the only notable development being me and Grant winning the fancy-dress competition. Our prize? A single shot each. Our pubs really were shite.

Closing time at the com would inevitably result in everyone standing outside smoking and on the hunt for someone having an after-party. Closing time was at midnight, and no-one wants to finish their night then. Most of us would continue until we passed out or until we heard the dreaded tweets of birds outside a party window. The heralds of your impending comedown.

I ended up going to a party in Westford with my girlfriend's brother. There were five of us, three boys and two girls, sitting in a dilapidated living room, all in our costumes, drinking, taking lines of speed and listening to tunes. 118 man, Freddie Mercury, a giant hotdog, a sexy nurse and a sexy cat (girls' costumes are lovely to look at but terribly unimaginative), all huddled round a glass table surrounded by squalor. Dali couldn't have painted a more surreal sight.

Freddie Mercury was my girlfriend's brother, Gordon, an overexcited guy, who up close looked like someone better viewed from far away. He was only happy if he had people who would party with him and pay him attention. The hotdog was Ian, a quiet boy who wouldn't say boo to a goose but got louder the higher points proof his blood got. The sexy nurse was neither sexy nor a nurse. If she was, then she would be Harold Shipman's go-to choose.

Abby, the sexy cat, was indeed sexy, with natural feline eyes, wide alert and mischievous. The extent of her costume was a black cat ear hairband and whiskers painted on her ears. Her little black dress was barely containing her chest, so no one really noticed her costume anyway. She had a sick sense of humour, like me (she once had Bradley from "S Club 7" to a party in her Aberdeen flat. She made him spend the entire night drinking and talking to people from a tiny cupboard under her stairs as he was "naughty"). We took to each other straight away.

Out of nowhere, the left side of my face exploded in pain. I was hit so hard my fake handlebar moustache pinged off my face and flew across the room to stick on the opposite wall.

Frank had been hunting me all night and had managed to get hold of Grant at a different party. I've been told, when questioned about my whereabouts, he folded like a deckchair, and he told Frank exactly where I was. Frank let himself in the girl's house, walked through to the living room and gave me a haymaker to the face without saying a word to anyone. He then followed up his initial punch with an upper cut to my moustache-less face, fracturing my eye socket, breaking my nose in two places and knocking me out.

He grabbed me by my vest and started dragging me to the front door, all still without saying a word. The rest of the party were too shocked and scared of Frank to even question him. He had a fearsome reputation for violence, and to get on the wrong side of a him was a grudge against you forever. Frank was tall with slabs of muscle and good-looking features that had sinister undertones. You were always uneasy in his presence. He didn't need to threaten anyone in the room; they all knew what he would do to grasses, and they were all shitebags anyway.

"What the fuck are you doing, Frank? Leave him alone," said Abby, the only actual friend in that party, and thank fuck she had a spine.

"The wee cunt's coming with me," he said in his quick Gypsy accent. Imagine Brad Pitt in Snatch.

He had dragged me outside into the garden before I came to my senses. I tried to pull free of his grip and leg it, but he punched me in the back of the head and I hit the deck. I was hoisted up and put in a vice-like headlock.

"Try to run and I'll hit you again, you fucking fool." Drunk, high, dazed and concussed, I complied and let him drag me along, still in a headlock. His house was just around the corner from the party, so he didn't have to drag me far. Once inside his house, he threw me on the floor and locked his front door.

Interlude

March

I am high as I write this now. Lovely coke injected in the crook of my arm. On my tattoo of a rampant lion, so to hide any tram lines. I also have Goblin's inside me and all is good in the world. When I feel like this I never want to stop. I'm happy to be a junkie forever. I just need to find a way to not drag my family into my madness. Drugs equals no voices, no overthinking everything, no urge to kill yourself with every item or obstacles you pass. Drugs make me feel how I think everyone feels who doesn't have monsters in their closet and in their head. I feel normal but I know it will kill me. Is being normal worth the price? Is living but fighting a constant battle in your head even living? My mind is like walking on a knife edge every day. Death on both sides and agony to keep your balance.

   PS. Is there is anything worse than having a spider loose in your room when you're trying to sleep?

I sit here sober and bouncing my son on my knee. I have been clean two weeks; I am happy and at peace. The only time I can remember being truly happy is when I am with my kids or high on drugs. That can't be it for my life. There must be something more out there for me. My sole purpose in life can't just be to reproduce and pass on my faulty, fucked up genes.

I have been off it three weeks now and I'm down the river with my eldest son There is a big salmon ladder next to the distillery by my parents' house we call the sloosh. My son has loved going to it ever since he was old enough to walk. Even though I have been clean three weeks, I am still feeling the repercussions of the drugs. I am due six hundred to a dealer but I'm all out of tricks. I can't juggle any more debt. I have no favours left to call in and I have no money to even attempt to win more by gambling. I hate the drugs, but they love me. The rushing sound of the water keeps calling to me. Primal sounds of my own death. I miss drugs and I'm scared.

April

I have been staying with my parents a month now, as my wife cannot handle my erratic behaviour any more. At the beginning, I was still using heavily and using every trick in the book to hide it from my mum and dad. Pills behind books on the bookshelves, needles behind picture frames, dead drops of drugs in the woods. Eventually it became too much effort and I gave up. I have slowly managed to stitch my shattered mind back together and although I have fallen off the wagon a few times, I am still taking ninety per cent less drugs than I was.

The voices still scream at me and every second stretches to an eternity. Also, no one can get me angry like my parents: they make things so much harder and are in essence pulling at the threads of my mind. I had to go up to mine to de-flea my cat the other day, and my mum insisted on chaperoning me in case I took the syringe used to spray the de-flea on the cat and use it for god knows what, as it has no needle. I need home. Rehab is for quitters, recovery is painful, and redemption is for the repentant.

I always wanted to be an explorer, but I was born too late for it. Death is the final frontier. The unknown, as no one has ever returned. And I crave the unknown… Death is but a door.

I am on new tablets from the psychiatrist for schizophrenia and I hate them. I have shut myself off from everyone but my kids. The voices whispering to me have become my only friends. We are all one. Our life's energy is split from the whole and they want me to re-join the fold. I can feel everything. If I relax my eyes, I can see individual molecules floating in the air, feel the vibrations of everything around me. I long for death, for my vibration to slow and match the deep resonance of the whole.

What is it to die? The atheists among us will quote that you did not mind the untold eons before your birth, so why should you mind after you die?

But perhaps now is the time before my birth, and upon my death I will truly be born.

Before I got my wife back years ago, my cheating was the worst. I was a cunt. It wasn't that I didn't love or respect my wife, it was that I didn't love or respect myself. I have always hated myself but my wife makes me a better person. There has never been anyone for me since she took me back, but when my cheating went extinct my drug taking flourished. I don't know why I need to fuck up everything, I don't deserve happiness.

How Can You Dream If You Haven't Been to Sleep?

"Admit it, you wee cunt! Admit shagging Sarah!" Sarah was Frank's partner and mother to his kids. She was also Grants's cousin, and me and Grant had been at a party with her a few weeks previous. Frank was in and out of that party as well and kept jokingly saying, "I hope you're giving Sarah plenty of orgasms, Marty," so it must have been a worry in the back of his mind already.

I have never been near Sarah, and for once in my life I was completely blameless. An innocent caught up in a paranoid fantasy.

Little did I know that that another local boy, James, had been winding Frank up earlier in the night. "I can't believe you are letting Marty get away with shagging your bird." Me and James got on okay, but he just liked causing chaos wherever he went.

"Frank, I swear I've never been near her; I'm not that stupid," I slurred. He marched me through to the kitchen where he pulled his t-shirt off to display his bulging chest and arm muscles, reached over my shoulder to pull a kitchen knife out of its block and uttered a single word.

"Beg."

"Look, Frank, I swear man. I did not do anything."

My head was still spinning from the blows, and I was still steaming and high. I don't think I realised how much danger I was actually in.

"Fucking get on your knees and beg." To my eternal credit,

I never got down to beg.

"I'm not getting on my knees to beg for something I didn't do." He dropped the knife and punched me in the lip, bursting it and spraying blood everywhere. He then grabbed me and launched me into his kitchen wall, leaving a Martin-shaped hole in the plasterboard like a fucking loony tunes cartoon when I crumbled to the floor.

For the second time in the space of half an hour I was knocked unconscious.

I awoke to the sound of screaming. I was lying on Frank's living room carpet, surrounded by empty cider bottles and fag burns.

"You have killed him, Frank, you have fucking killed him!" Sarah was standing at the top of their stairs looking dishevelled and holding their kid, who was bawling his eyes out.

I tried to sit up and my head spun. I felt as if I were moving through a thick fog and my left eye was swollen shut. Frank noticed that I was awake and gave me a toe poke to the ribs for good measure, knocking the wind out of me.

"You're lucky you ain't dead, boy," he said. Not so much that I was lucky to be alive but implying that I was lucky I wasn't dead, or he would hurt me more. The fucking idiot.

He picked me up by the throat one-handed, slammed me against the front door and started to throttle the life out of me.

"You will never get out of here if you don't admit what you did," he said, calm as you like.

"Let him go, Frank, he hasn't done anything!" Sarah screamed hysterically, just about making herself heard over her baby.

It was then I noticed a third voice shouting, adding to the madness. It was Abby on the other side of the front door, shouting through the letterbox. "The police are on their way, Frank. Let him go!"

31

"Please, Frank, please," sobbed Sarah.

"Last chance," Frank whispered as he squeezed my throat tighter. I was fading out of consciousness again but managed to rasp out, "I didn't do it."

It was like a switch went off in Frank's head. "Okay, pal." He let go of my neck, unlocked the bolt on the front door next to my head, opened it then spun me round and gently shoved me outside into Abby and a cool breeze. I heard the door softly close behind me.

Abby quickly half-walked half-dragged me out of his garden. "We need to go, Marty. The police ain't actually coming." Abby might have been the only one to help me, but she still wasn't stupid enough to call the police. That would have meant months of harassment for her and her family so she wouldn't testify against Frank in court. A lifetime if he got convicted.

What I did next is one of the stupidest things I have ever done. I pushed Abby away, shuffled back to Frank's house and chapped on the door.

Frank answered. "Yes, Marty?" he said, like a waiter taking my order and looking for a good tip.

"I think I dropped my phone in yours; can I have it back?"

"No bother, bud, two seconds," he said and disappeared into the house. He returned a minute later with my cheap Nokia phone. "There you are, pal, see ya later." And once again he softly closed his door.

I limped back towards Abby. "What the fuck is wrong with you, Martin?"

I had no idea.

Choices

My eyes shot open, and I was surrounded with stars once again, the horror show of my death still frozen in time below my feet. Rand and Bill were both standing in front of me, one wearing a grin like a scythe, the other a mask of stars and galaxies, dying and been reborn, shifting across his features.

"Oooo, I liked him," said Rand. Each syllable that wormed its way out of his mouth seemed to hit me in the face, shooting pain into the places Frank had injured me in the memory.

"Why is this happening? Why me?" I was sick to my stomach, and I felt a dull ache in my face, almost a ghost of the pain I had endured from Frank sixteen years ago.

"I suppose you could say we have a wager of sorts. There is no point in us doing this with every soul who passes through our world. Most people's choices throughout their lives have already determined their final destination. You still coast through life in an ambiguous grey area. You stand on a knife edge, a crossroads at twilight. Which makes it oh so exciting for a gambling man." Rand's eyes glittered, and his teeth shone as he spoke.

"What if I refuse to play?"

"Then you die now. You break your wife's heart. Tyler will never get over it and Flynn will grow up never knowing his father. Your soul will float through purgatory forever if you are lucky, if not its turtles all the way down," Rand gloated.

"So, what is it to be? Did this experience play a part in the grotesque scene below us? Tick tock tick tock."

"No," I replied quickly. Not out of pride or arrogance, trying

33

to show I wasn't scared of the experience. Because let me tell you, when that knife was waving in my face, I was fucking terrified. I said no because I knew I had a void inside me long before I was kidnapped. The feeling has always been there. A foreboding of horrible things to come, a permanent feeling of impending doom. It can be pushed to the back of my mind and I can paint over the cracks, but I can never escape it.

"Excellent," Rand said gleefully, clapping his hands. "Told you, he would fuck this up."

"You chose wrong, Martin," Bill said, and the stars in his face seemed to dim. The rotation of the galaxies slowed. He seemed disappointed in me, and I felt I had let him down somehow. Even though he was part architect of this fucked up game I was playing I had a gut feeling he was on my side. "You may not have realised it at the time but facing your own morality that night took the fear of death from you. You lost all feeling of self-preservation. Can you not see how this contributed to your self-destruction?"

"Time is short, but death is infinitely tall, Marty, and it waits for no one. We must move on quickly. As you can see below, time may have slowed for your mortal flesh but has not stopped completely," said Rand.

I looked down at my body and my convulsion seemed to have stopped. My body was now lying flat on the bathroom floor and the pool of blood had spread, giving me the look of having a crimson halo. My wife was on her knees next to me, as out of place in this scene as an injured swallow caught in the jaws of a wolf. I didn't deserve her.

"On to the next," Bill said, placing a finger gently on the centre of my forehead. "Please don't rush your answer next time. Look inward and you will know the truth."

My eyes closed and my reality spun.

34

Is This a Studenty Place?

I miss Edinburgh, I miss the pubs, I miss the fringe, I miss the cow gate and I fucking miss the pubic triangle. I miss the noise of the city as I fell asleep. University was barely a factor to me the whole time I lived there. Just an inconvenience between parties and student life.

Most of all I miss my final years when I lived with Carly. How to describe Carly? She was and is my best friend, closer than a sister, as she knows and has taken part in all my escapades. I met her when I was about nineteen and going out with her best friend. It may be because of this I have never looked at her as anything other than my confidante. She is good looking, short, dark-haired and has been the voice of reason to me so many times. My fun-loving Jiminy cricket. We both recognise in one other something that is missing in each other's lives. A friendship that will last forever.

She comes from an even dingier remote town than Alness, so she jumped at the chance to move in with me when I told her my last flat mate had grown sick of my antics. (The straw that broke the camel's back was when I hid a raw kipper in his lunch bag and he didn't notice it till his lunch at work six hours later.) For two years, Carly and I were flatmates and, in that time, there was never a cross word between us, even though I kept the place in a constant state of bedlam. She was a female usher at my wedding, and she is engaged to a man I introduced to her in our flat. It was a talking point for years that they shared their first kiss less than an hour after I had taken him back to our flat from visiting the whores.

Carly and I would spend our weekends flitting from party to party, be it in Edinburgh or Glasgow. If it was in Glasgow, I would fire onto the M8 and get there in twenty minutes. I was an unbelievably reckless driver. The car would be abandoned at whatever student digs we had got invited to. Instead of finding somewhere to crash at the end of the night, we would get back in my car and fly it back to my flat. I used to say it was called KIT and always drove me home no matter how drunk I was. One night in Glasgow after a view gig and a night on the eccies, Mish and I, another of my closest friends, went to drive back to my flat. It had been snowing, so we needed to defrost the car. While scraping off the snow, Mish thought it would be funny to spray de-icer in my eyes.

"Ahhhh, fuck ya doing, you cunt? This burns like fuck."

"Scoosh scoosh, haha," was all his high mind could reply.

"Aye, well done, blind your fucking driver, ya mongo. Get in the fucking car." I hadn't even defrosted the windscreen properly yet, so I drove along the M8 at ninety miles per hour with my head hanging out the window Ace Ventura-style, eyes streaming with de-icer. It's a miracle we made it back to my flat alive.

I also drove home one night then forgot where I had parked in the morning. I spent a day walking around all my usual spots then phoned the police to report it stolen. Turns out I had abandoned it in a disabled bay, and it was impounded with a three hundred pounds fine to get it out. What a fucking idiot.

T in the Fucking P

The night before T in the Park, Carly and I threw a party, and by fuck it was a party. Instead of all our friends, who were going to T in the Park, getting up early in Alness and driving two hours to Balado, they came to ours the night before so they would have a more relaxed thirty-minute commute to the festival in the morning. Or so we thought.

Twenty-odd people were crammed into our two-bedroom flat, and a convoy of cars took up every student parking space for the building. It was bedlam. Our flat was on the ground floor and had a sliding door to the meagre garden then the carpark. People were spilling out of the flat, smoking and getting the craic.

The police were first called because of the noise and one boy took umbrage to this. He was convinced that it was the upstairs flat that called the police, so he put on a Bin Laden mask I had lying around from Halloween and tried to climb up onto their balcony from our patio to give them a fright. The police arrived again stating the laughable offence of a terrorist attack as the reason for the call. The whole fucking room began pissing themselves when the poor cop had to say that to me at the door. We were told to disperse, so everyone got in their cars and left, did a short trip round the block till the police had fucked off then came back to the flat and the madness continued.

I was literally putting fires out all over the party. I could have killed a boy when he tried to make popcorn but left his phone in the microwave, nearly causing the kitchen to burn down. He was

37

so upset at the ruin of his brand-new iPhone that I couldn't stay mad at him for long. I also had to break down our only bathroom door, as Mac' nRae, another pal, had gone to be sick, locked the door behind him then passed out on the floor. Situations like this are what I have sought all my adult life. I didn't even mind the debauchery and destruction of our flat and joyfully zipped from problem to problem in my protective cocoon of drink and drugs.

Leaving for T in the Park the next morning was a mission, but the excitement of the festival to come dulled any hangover we all felt. The ultimate Friday feeling.

The sun had not even reached its zenith yet, and the temperature was a sweltering twenty-five degrees. Unheard of in Scotland. I was trying to drag a cart full to the brim with drink through a field of churned mud whilst carrying a tent and a sparse bag of clothes. This was the obstacle course all revellers had to navigate each year for T in the Park, the final test of the course being playing it cool as you crossed the security checkpoint manned by police and sniffer dogs. I had wrapped my speed and eccies in several layers of cling film then orange peels to throw the dogs off the scent and finally hidden in a half-full bottle of hair gel.

"I don't think I'm gonna make it," Andy said one hundred yards from the entrance. Andy was my best friend and the only cunt I have ever known to wear cowboy boots regardless of the occasion… in fucking Scotland. We had been best friends ever since we met one day in the woods by my house ten years ago. We were both on the hunt for a good tree to build a swing from. His skinny frame was perfect for climbing the thinner trees and branches to tie ropes.

I think the treetops are his natural habitat, as he resembles a twig. He has shoulder-length hair and a patchy beard, as he thinks this is rock 'n' roll. This is as far as he takes the rock 'n' roll stereotype, as he is a rare breed amongst my friends, as he has never touched a drug in his life. I respect him far more for this than if he actually took them. He refuses all peer pressure even though he has no particular reason to not take them. He just doesn't like being a sheep. We were still forcing him to mule some of our gear over the border regardless of his abstinence.

"Fuck off, ya runt, I'm dragging all the cans an' sinking further into this bog with every step. You are like Legolas on the snow over there."

This was our third T in the Park, so we were smug as fuck when we breezed through security. A fuck you to the man. Rebels without a clue. T in the Park's campsite is a large expanse of field, pristine in the morning, a tabula rasa only to be churned into a small village of debauchery come nightfall, sin and excess etched into its surface. It was still quite early, so we managed to get a good camping spot near the Duracell Powerhouse. This is rave tent that plays on into the night once the main park is closed. Several texts to other groups of friends and they arrived in dribs and drabs to set all our tents up in a circle with a big space in the middle for us to similarly line our camping chairs up and sesh together.

Freddy, one of my mates from footy, was there. He is notorious for winding people up and giving cheek. He is a short fat guy with rosy cheeks and the beginnings of an alcoholic's nose. Even though he could be the brunt of many a jokes himself, he tears into everyone relentlessly. A poor, quiet boy, Oliver, had arrived, set up his tent then gone to one of the numerous burger vans dotted about the site. Freddy suddenly declared he needed a shite. He whipped down his shorts and reversed into Oliver's tent, zipped it up so just his face was showing and began to squeeze.

We could tell by his facial expressions and his moans that this was no easy task he was undertaking. He had a face like a bulldog licking pish off a nettle. He finished, unzipped, wiped his arse with baby wipes, zipped the tent back up then sat back down with the group like nothing had happened. Oliver didn't check his tent when he got back, and we all went straight to the arena. That shite was cooking in his tent for a good nine hours in a rare Scottish heatwave.

When we returned that night, everyone was waiting for the inevitable. When Oliver finally unzipped his tent, there was a blast of smell that could have stripped paint off a car. He screamed like he had seen a dead body and turned a strange shade of green. Poor cunt. I let him sleep in mine an Andy's tent, as I was in no fit state for rest. I had taken five eccies over the course of the day and was twitching to dance. I headed to the Duracell Powerhouse to join the rest of the swinging jaws like a room full of pendulums.

The Friday was a warm-up, Saturday a dress rehearsal and Sunday the main attraction for me. The View were headlining King Tut's tent on Sunday.

The View were the main reason for my attendance at T in the Park that year. If there was a soundtrack to my life, it would be The View. I remember the exact moment I first heard one of their songs. I was working as a youth worker in Alness and "Wasted Little DJs" came on the radio. I have never had a feeling like it since. A feeling of belonging. That this music was made especially for me. Since then, I have been to over forty of their gigs, following them around Scotland. I dealt the bassist speed in Inverness, got pished on by a hooligan in Edinburgh and made it onto a live DVD at the Barras in Glasgow. Camera pans past me in the front row and I'm out of my face, chewing Mish's ear. Me and two of my best mates, Dave and Mish, have tattoos of the same lyrics.

"Dreams, romance and excess." Words to live by.

Saturday was scorching hot; half of my pals went bright red instantly. The Scottish suntan. We were all sitting in our circle, drinking cans in the sun and ribbing each other. Dave, Carly's future husband, was rolling about fighting with his older brother, Evan. Mish was talking shite to Andy about some people they heard shagging last night and trying to guess who it was, and Freddy was tearing into Ally, another quiet boy, about being a virgin. I knew for a fact that he was not a virgin. I had picked the girl he lost his virginity to by throwing a ping pong ball at her head in a brothel in Thailand last summer. All my close mates were there, the sun was shining and I was full of drink and drugs. The void inside was nearly filled. Everyone was happy and on the sesh. Life was perfect.

Mish was trying to take the piss out of my tattoos, as I have a shitty Chinese symbol on my leg. I got it in a van at T in the Park the previous year. I was told it means happy, but I have asked every Chinese person I see, and they have no idea. I showed it in a Chinese shop before, and he served me chicken fried rice.

"Just looks like a squashed spider to me, ya cunt," Mish, shouted at me.

He has his date of birth in Roman numerals on his wrist and he is slightly larger than my clothes horse build so I fire back, "That's no your date of birth; that's your shirt size."

Winding each other up is a national pastime so he tries a different tactic.

"I bet ya you won't get another one this year. Na, fuck that:

41

I dare you to get a piercing."

"Only if you get one as well." I had no fear of needles or pain at this point and in hindsight a healthy phobia of needles would have served me well.

"Fine. Soon as we get in, aye."

"Aye." I was pretty sure he would shite bag it anyway.

We headed into the arena early with our CamelBacks full of vodka and the mixture of your choice. Pockets bulging full of drugs. The security to get in the arena was less tight that the initial one for the campsite but you still shat it if you saw a cop with a sniffer dog. You couldn't turn around either, as that would just be an admission of guilt and they would chase you.

One sat down next to me before at a previous festival. "Who's a good boy then? Are you smelling my dogs? Aww, that must be it." My patter with the dog didn't impress the cops one bit, and my decency was violated. I got the old rubber glove treatment and every orifice searched. He was rooting around my bum like a cave explorer but came up empty handed. I was admitted to the arena a changed man. Worth it though, as they didn't find the eccies stashed in my foreskin.

Our entry to the T in the Park arena was smooth, so we headed to the tattoo and piercing place. It's pretty much just a greasy burger van where you pick what you want on the menu and are taken round back. Mish, wanting to one-up me, said he would go first. He was taken round back by what can only be described as an ogre. No health and safety standards here. Mish was only gone five minutes before he came out proudly displaying a surface piercing on his wrist.

"What the fuck is that?" I burst out laughing. "That to hang your keys on?"

Easy win for me, but I wanted to blow him out of the water.

Short of getting my knob done, which would probably be impossible with the serious case of "pilly willy" I had going on (drugs had shrunk my knob to a Tic Tac), I went for the tongue piercing.

On the morning of day two of a major festival.

I let Mish come round with me to watch. He was horrified just thinking about it. I was drunk at the time so was very blasé and showing off. I hardly felt the needle going through my tongue, as I had rubbed a bit of speed on it beforehand. I was done in five minutes as well. Regardless of how dirty the ogre was, he was efficient. A rate of impaling twelve spaced out revellers an hour.

The only aftercare I got was a grunt – "There may be some swelling" – and I was pushed out of the burger van. It didn't seem swollen, so I thought I had got away with it. We re-joined the main group when they entered the arena and Mish was not impressed so we agreed that we were both daft cunts, took more drugs and forgot all about our new metal wear. I love Mish, we are so alike and who the fuck would not want a friend that tries to winds you up at any given moment anyway? A group of girls had joined us now, so the twenty or so of us wandered from band to band, living live to the full.

When it started to get dark, we found ourselves in the sideshows. Me and another boy picked a waltzer-looking thing to go on. I thought it just spun us in a circle so had the brilliant idea of taking poppers on it (a sex aid, or room odoriser, depending on where you get it from. It gives you a head rush when you inhale deeply, and it relaxes all your body muscles, so your arse swallows the couch). I pulled out the bottle and went to take a sniff, but just as I did, the ride took an unexpected twist. Paul, the boy sitting next to me, said, "Marty, I'm pretty sure we're upside down."

The whole bottle was emptied down my nose and into my right eye. When I got off the ride, my eye was stuck shut, swollen and all the skin inside my nose was burnt red.

Some rush though.

My eye was so bad I had to spend the next hour in the medical tent with nurses running saline water into my eye. There was some poor space cadet next to me on a drip and clearly tripping. He was ginger, mangy-looking with teeth like a row of condemned houses and was pishing sweat. He kept shouting that he was Hitler and needed to walk Blondi. Not waiting to hang about until he decided my swollen nose looked Jewish, I insisted on leaving the tent. I just made it in time to meet my group at the main stage to watch Kasabian close the Saturday night.

Interlude

May

A guy I knew from back in the day killed himself recently. He must have been going through what I am now. I feel an affinity with him and a respect that he had the courage of his convictions and saw them through to the end. I don't know if I'm a coward for not managing to kill myself or brave that I have held off. Either way, I am jealous of him, his battle is over and I am stuck with Stockholm Syndrome in my own addictions. I wish him well.

I cracked, or slipped, or slipped into the crack. First pay check and I'm back to my old ways. Shooting up in the toilets of my new job. I had never really quit, I was just forced into submission by lack of funds and availability. I'm not sure I even want to quit. The thought of being sober is terrifying. I can't trust myself with anything. Time with my kids is the only respite. They are my guardian angels. I don't know why I have them; they are too clean for my filth, too pure for me. I fear I will corrupt them. Not intentionally, never that, but just by my presence. I am a black hole.

The claws are in again. I worked so hard to get home to my long-suffering wife and my kids, but it's so easy to fall back into bad habits. And I have no excuse this time. My psychiatrist has given me tablets for schizophrenia, and the voices have retreated. I know they are still there. I can hear them sometimes, but they are dormant. The allure of drugs is not though. It wasn't the voices that drove me to it this time; it wasn't my bipolar; it wasn't anything but me. My disposition to cause chaos. To do what I've been told not to. Everything is on the line for me and I still roll the dice.

I hate myself.

What is time? Have I done this before, and will I do it again? Does it matter now that I have done it once and time is infinite? The past, future and present are one, so my act of overdose has and always will be happening. Do I believe this, or is it just an excuse I tell myself to stay a junkie? Why can't I have a middle ground? On one hand, I'm a nervous, depressed, suicidal guy who can't find joy in anything. On the other hand, there is a toxic junkie. Give me drugs and I am happy. The pain disappears.

Why can't there be a hybrid? A guy who is content with life and doesn't feel the need to destroy everything and everyone around him. Why can't I do things in moderation? Just get a hobby and not have it turn into an all-consuming obsession. Just get slightly drunk and not have it led to shooting up coke and on the hunt for any party that will have me. Just go slightly insane…

Life is precious to me, but I long to re-join the whole. The all-encompassing energy that we are part of but not part of at the same time. Separated at birth and reunited at death. I would not take my own life: that would be a sin in my eyes. I say a sin as if I believe in a specific deity, and even if I did, I would spit in his eyes. But pushing my addictions to the limits and overdosing… that is no sin. I would be cheating the system. It's nice to live this way, without any fear of death. Liberating.

Does destiny exist? Surely, I was not born to be a junkie? The future is malleable, I can do anything or be anything I want. It is only me who is stubborn and refuses to change my ways. Wallowing in my own misery. King of my hill of dirt and despair.

I think too much. I dwell on things and turn an imagined slight in a conversation into a monster in my head. Then silence it with drugs. And who do I blame? Myself? Certainly not.

My partner? My parents? Evolution? God?

Either way, I have taken fire from heaven and used it to burn down my house. Fuck I am rambling again, I really am losing my grip on reality.

June

I am back home with my boys. God knows why my wife let me home after what I did, but I think she regrets it now. She lives in constant fear that I am going to do it again, and we are at each other's throats because of it. I know I will forever be in the wrong, but I can't just lie down for every argument. I can see the resentment grow faster than my son. We will end up staying together for the kids. Worst-case scenario, as I can't live without her. Soulmate is banded about, but that is what she means to me. I haven't looked at another woman in years for her so surely I can give up drugs for her.

Being a junkie is wearing jumpers in the sunshine to hide the bruises on your arms

Relapse! Caught like a rat in a trap. Surprise drug test and I am back to square one again. Well, not square one. I'm not kicked to the secular hell that is my parents' house. Banished to my boyhood room with all the implications that come with that. No, I'm allowed to stay at home. I think they were expecting this. They were prepared. Test twenty-four hours earlier and I was golden. C'est la vie. It had to happen sometime. I was never going to stay clean forever. My soul is too dirty for that.

I know it's not something to be proud of, but fuck am I good at shooting up. Never miss a vein, never leave track marks; this train driver is a prodigy. Even at the end of a bag, when I have tremors so bad, I can't type on my phone legibly, fwoop, straight into the bloodstream it goes, no need to show your tickets, folks, final destination – my heart. Why is it black?

Now that I'm back on it, I've taken to keeping my needle tucked down the side of my trousers, like a gun. Draw, motherfucker. I keep it on me at all times in case it's found and taken off me like it has been before. It has become... precious to me, ha. Gollum, Gollum.

I can feel the demons calling to arms in my psyche. The vultures circling. Or to drop the stupid metaphors, my mind beginning to snap. Unable to bow any further from the pressures of the world. Pressures other people seem to take in their stride. I have a friend from work who always seems so happy, so infuriatingly happy all the time. He is like a Springer Spaniel from a Disney movie. Why can't I be like him? Why can't I take pleasure from the small things in life? This is why I run and try to cloak myself in a cloud of narcotics. I am sad and bored, bored of being sad and sad because I am bored.

I ask myself all the time how it came to this. Why did I do this to myself? Do I want to die? Do I hate myself? Are the voices that bad? Are drugs worth it? What about my sons? Repeated grillings, day after day. The answer to most of them is yes, but that's not the real answer. The real answer is boredom. Life bores me, everything about it. Everything from work to hobbies to my family. It is all monotonous, a set path already preordained by the upper class. And I don't mean the upper class as in the toffs at Eton playing their king-of-the-hill game, I mean their masters, who hide behind the veil of companies and media. The hidden hands that shape the world.

I have too little motivation to try and break these chains, but I will move mountains to chase a high. It is better to rule in hell than serve in heaven, and I rule my own personal hell with an iron syringe. I only feel alive when I am high on something, be it alcohol, coke or adrenaline. So yes, boredom. Boredom drives me to do dangerous things and take dangerous substances, regardless of the detriment to my life and regardless how fleeting the thrill. Idle hands and all that...

I look down at my hands, rose tattooed on one hand, skull on the other. The perfect juxtaposition of my mind. Sanity and madness. Life and death. Regardless, they are both shaking.

I dream sometimes of when I was last content. Quiet. Silence. The absence of all sound. There is nothing like being in the forest, surrounded by a fresh dump of powder. The snow muffles even the smallest noise. I am in the middle of a back-country piste in the Rocky Mountains all on my own. My two roommates I was boarding with have long since left me behind. At my insistence. I needed this. It's my happy place, my fortress of solitude. When the world screams and the voices claw, this is where I try to retreat to. The calm I try to muster in my head. A pure snapshot of content in my otherwise life of malcontent. Alone in nature for miles around. And silence.

I've always just thought I had one of those faces cunts wanted to try and change, but I don't think that any more. Now I just think it's my attitude people have tried to change. Trying to pop my bubble of arrogance with a few well-placed punches. I see all my choices and actions in fresh light, and I don't like what I see. I hate myself and want to die.

Why have you set yourself up as the antagonist of your own story? You could be the hero. The knight in shining armour, or the damsel in distress, depending on your proclivities. But you

49

are the hag with the poisoned apple. Tainting every action, you make. You need to change your perspective on life to have a hope of happiness. I know these facts, but I am powerless to change them. Drugs hold me hostage and I have Stockholm syndrome.

For the first year and a half of my marriage, I was sedated or high. I was an average father and a terrible husband. It only took me to die for me to actually try. Not coast along ignoring all my failings in a haze of narcotics. Ignorance is bliss, but I was neither ignorant of my shortcomings, nor was burying my head in the sand bliss. Apathy is not a crime I am guilty of. I am ashamed of what I was and what I have become. I am trying to be better for my family, but I don't think I deserve it. Drugs are the easy way out but also the hardest. God, I miss them, the simplicity of only having one goal. Having the same thoughts and the same feelings when you wake up and go to sleep. Comfortably numb.

How can you live a normal life when you think of death as an adventure?

I love knowledge, or at least the pursuit of it in its purest form. It's what made me a precocious reader, with *The Lord of the Rings* under my belt before I was six, to twenty-five years later reading the complete works of Walt Whitman due a small reference whilst watching *Breaking Bad* and indulging my drug-dealing fantasy. After floating around aimless in my early teens, I missed education, so it is one of the reasons I decided to study nursing. I made it two years into the degree before I quit.

Twenty years later, I discovered what a joke it was. What kind of nursing degree lets a student get to the end of their second year without teaching them that drugs must always be shot towards the heart and that air bubbles are inconsequential! Only when I became an addict did I learn the intricacies of intravenous drugs, how to find a vein and how air bubbles shot into a vein and not an artery will always pass through the lungs and remove said air bubble as opposed to going straight to the brain and causing the poor junkie to have an embolism.

I kept the habit of flicking the syringe to remove bubbles after learning this, because in my fucked-up head I thought I looked cooler, like some vigilante paramedic on American TV, saving the world one shot of cocaine at a time. My university course must have been terrible, or the more likely scenario, I was just a terrible student at the time and a much more avid scholar when it came to getting myself fucked up.

You may think I am writing this as a survivor, as a testimony to the madness. I am not. I have survived nothing. I am in the middle of the maelstrom, clinging to anything that offers refuge. Writing this is cathartic, so I write. A pen is very like a needle though, and I know it is only a matter of time.

I have a superiority complex, and I hate myself for it.

Is anything real, if I see one world and you see another? If I feel one thing from the same stimulus and you feel another? Can anything be trusted? My senses can betray me. Who's to say the voices I hear are not real and it's the silence you hear that is the lie? I'm submitting to the sweeter sound.

I have had the same alarm on my phone for the past fifteen years, moved from phone to phone as they have evolved. Andrew WK, "Party Hard". It was subconsciously picked at first then consciously kept. Shows what I thought I was. In the end I became a sordid parody of myself.

I ran an experiment tonight, with me as the willing guinea

pig. Stay away from cocaine, my family say; calm it on the gear, I get from my pals. Fair enough: let's find something else. I ordered meth online, just a gram. It's only an experiment, you see, and I got stuck in late one night with my family tucked up in bed. I was expecting an exhilarating rush, like the first time you take any other drug. I crash-coursed in the new chemicals I had built up no tolerance for.

I was let down. It kept me awake. I certainly looked like a space cadet when I locked eyes with myself in the mirror. But no rush, no euphoria. *Breaking Bad* is tainted for me now. All it gave me was a yearning, a longing for cocaine. Like when you are fucking a girl but imagining it's someone else.

Maybe the meth I got was just shit. Maybe I took it wrong. (I made sure I snorted and smoked the lot so I wouldn't be tempted to go to a pharmacist the next day to finish it off.) Or maybe my heart is broken, and only a reconciliation with my long-lost lover can mend it.

I saw an old mate from school the other night whom I have not seen in years. He was deep in the drugs. Former muscles wasted away, hollow cheeks and pinprick pupils. I knew what he was on straight away when we got chatting. It was like looking into a time machine to what I was a few months ago.

"Mr Douglas, how you doing? Heard you were no well for a bit?"

"You ken why I was no well, and what I was into, pal, was in deep. What you on the night?" He would know exactly, what I had been up to.

"Just the sniff. Yourself?"

"No, the smoke?" I said with a grin. "Your eyes are brown 'cos you're full of shite, haha"

"Na, I'm off it." He smirked. I knew fine it was crack he was

52

on. We can spot one another instantly. Like Vietnam vets could identify fellow survivors of the Viet Cong.

"Aye, you know yourself I'm not the one to speak to about that problem, haha," he said with a wink.

The implication was there, dropped subtly in a crowded shop. I could get whatever I wanted off him. Join him in the night's escapades. It took no small amount of willpower to walk out of the shop. I Was jealous of him but have been off coke for a month and didn't want to start back-peddling into the whirlpool again. The fact I was loaded on goblins during this crisis of character only emphasised the strength of character I showed in my eyes. The next morning, I heard he was stabbed three times trying to bump another dealer. I took this as a sign.

Dreams, Romance and Excess

I awoke Sunday morning with a splitting headache, a crusty eye, a burnt and blocked nose and a tongue five times its normal size. I have never had a hangover like it.

I crawled on all fours out of my tent, trying to move my head as little as possible, into another blistering summer day. My hangover had kept me comatose well past midday. Everyone had been out drinking for several hours, so I was going to have to play catch up.

"Haha, look at the nick of you. Did you try to eat a wasp's nest?" laughed Dave.

"Cunt looks like the elephant man," Andy said as I lowered myself into the camping chair next to him.

I tried unsuccessfully to smoke a fag for ten minutes before giving up in a huff and pouring myself a large vodka to try and lighten my mood.

"Want a straw?" Andy said.

"Fuck ofth," I replied as I slobbered my drink. The drunker I got, the less I cared about my face. Andy took my mind off my injuries with a spectacle I will never forget and which I spoke about at length in my best man speech at his wedding, several years later.

He got himself steaming and did his usual antics of running about naked. Running through other people's campsites to our delight. Our own personal streaker who we would set upon passing groups of campers like a fucked-up Pokémon. Andy returned from one of his streaking escapades with a tube used to pump up a lilo bed.

"Bet, I can chug a cider with my arse."

Cunt is not right in the head. It took him a good twenty minutes to convince Dave to stick the tube up his arse, hold it aloft and pour a cider down it. The tube was inserted prison-style, with not even a bit of spit for lube. To be fair, Andy took it like a man. I still have a picture somewhere of Dave pouring a cider down the tube with Andy lying on the ground, legs at a quarter to three. A T in the Park enema.

My facial condition improved dramatically, and when I managed to hock up a lump of phlegm half the size of my head, I spat it into the middle of our circle to the amazement of my mates.

"Could play football with that thing, ya minging bastard," Dave laughed. My airways were clear again, and I could see out of my eye. I could feel my face deflating the minute I got it out. Game on, let's do this, I thought. We all filled our CamelBacks and headed into the arena. I wanted to make sure we were in the King Tut's tent early, so we headed to the Bacardi bar situated right next to it. Mojitos and stomach cramps from the mint leaves all round for us all for the next four hours. When we started seeing the crowds gather to the tent, we headed in for the first main act, Pendulum.

Pendulum are a drum-and-bass act and attracted a medium-sized crowd to the tent. The temperature began to rise with the throng of bodies throwing themselves about to the tunes. Pendulum finished their set, and Jamie T came on. Jamie T would be a headliner on any other stage if The View were not booked on after. The tent now felt packed to capacity, and the temperature was tropical, the air moist and electric. Proper taps aff weather.

55

We snaked, pushed and squeezed our way to just behind the front row. Jamie T played through his set, the excitement rising with each song and the tent filling past bursting point. Jamie T closed his set with "Sheila" and the crowd singing every word back to him – "London!"

Finally, for me, The View came on, the Dundee Beatles. The crowd went mental. This was at the height of their fame, and their opening song, "Wasteland," electrified the crowd. During an instrument change, I noticed I was next to an older guy I knew from home who dabbled a bit in dealing . I got on with him okay, so naturally we greeted each other like long lost brothers, hugging each other topless, our sweaty bodies slapping together.

"Here, you want a key of coke?" He shouted to be heard among the sea of exuberance.

"Why not?" And he jammed near half a g of coke up my nose using his house key as a shovel. I sniffed and I was lifted to a higher plane of existence. Colours became brighter, the music became clearer, everyone in the milling crowd was my family, the press of bodies a lover's embrace.

At the end of every song, he shoved more coke up my hungry nostrils. The View closed their set with the usual "Shock Horror".

"I feel sorry for you, man. You have forgotten how to clap your hands!" Kyle, the frontman, wailed, and the whole crowd clapped their hands as one. The final clap of my hands and like the twang of a taught bowstring, I was fired from my young, carefree body into a middle-aged, worn-down junkie on the brink of death.

I Feel Sorry for You, Man

I was lying in water again. Only this time, I felt its cold grip, making me shiver. I stood up and my head swam. The stars were shooting across my vision in great streaks, comets dragging tails of agony. My face had started to swell and bleed. I raised my hand and could feel an open wound on my eyebrow.

"You are starting to feel the wounds of your body below," Bill said.

"Don't let your pain cloud your vision. So, once again I ask, did this lead to the below?"

I dared to look down again. My body was flat on my back now, my face unrecognisable. Just a mound of swollen flesh. My wife was gone, replaced by a paramedic, who was frozen mid-pull of the needle in my arm.

"Yes, yes it did." I felt bile rise in my throat, I don't know if from the pain or the sudden snap from euphoria to agony.

"Easy fucking choice considering he's addicted to coke," hissed Rand. "The first time he tries ching – such an obvious memory to pick."

"You set these rules. I abide by them." There was a touch of pride in Bill's voice, and for the first time I could see they were at odds. Rivals, not co-conspirators. Rand stalked towards me, and I was hit with a wave of heat, nearly enough to take away the chill that had set into my bones.

"That's the last easy choice you will get here. You are mine! Let me show you a little something before your next trip down memory lane."

The stars overhead changed hue and began bleeding a dark red light. Storm clouds raced across the sky and purple forks of lightening crack all around. The shallow water I was standing in coalesced into a thick fog. A fog I had seen before, had been running from for the past few months. Arms began reaching out to me, followed by heads and shoulders of faceless beings. Discordant moans filled the air. A chorus of agony and despair. I was frozen to the spot, unable to speak. I could barely draw breath.

"Nice, isn't it. My personal garden of Styx. They are all lost in death. The road to hell is paved with good intentions and bad choices. If you can't find your way in life, then you don't deserve a path to follow in death. This is the fork in the road, the dark clearing stumbled upon in the wood, false north, the end of a broken future. You will be joining them soon. Mark my words."

The fog began to dissipate, the sky cleared and the whispers died just as they did for me many times before when I took drugs. Rand's tone shifted from a benevolent tyrant to that of a jovial uncle. "I'm enjoying this more than I should. Shall we see what we have in store next? Once more unto the breach!"

"If we must," I sighed. The fear was in me now, fear I had not felt for most of my adult life. My apathy towards my death was well and truly gone. I wanted to live.

The stars spun, a tornado of lights, and I blacked out.

We'll Be Comin' Down the Road

The hardest thing in the world is taking a shite in a kilt, made worse by the fact I'm thirty thousand feet in the air and steaming drunk. The front of my kilt slips out between my teeth and falls into my stream of piss. "Fuck!"

I half-waddle back down the aisle and collapse into my seat next to a passed-out Tommy. Tommy is a handsome, gentle giant. The kind of good-looking Disney characters are, but he is too nice for his own good, and that's an invitation to get the piss ripped out of you in our group.

We are five hours into a twelve-hour flight from London to Sao Paulo, and we are all the worse for wear. We have all been drinking now for a good ten hours. I haven't even been to sleep yet, and I'm already rough. My balls are chaffed raw rubbing off my kilt. Wearing anything under your kilt is sacrilege, even on an eighteen-hour globe-spanning journey such as this. Clarting them in Vaseline is usually the answer, but alas, I left my travel jelly at home.

Something smacks into the back of my head and falls into my lap. It is an empty miniature wine bottle. I turn around to see my dad ginning at me a few rows back.

"Wake that boring, fat cunt up." My dad is a shortish man with bright silver hair that he has had since his mid-twenties, and a prominent nose. His nickname is either "the silver fox" or "brown tie". "Brown tie" refers to a sex move that he described, to my horror, to a group of my mates on a stag do. You get a girl to lie on her back, then you sit on her, dunking your balls in her mouth and simultaneously giving her a brown tie. His description of this to the stag was met with thunderous laughter and constant slagging to me that he had performed this manoeuvre on my mother.

His attention is immediately dragged away from me by his brother. My uncle is sitting next to him, a self-made millionaire who took to his old age disgracefully. Fat, bald, loud and funny, he is more of an older brother to me than an uncle. I call him Muncle as it eventually became abbreviated to after telling so many stories of him that started with "My uncle". I had never seen the pair of them so drunk.

I give Tommy a slap. "Wake up, ya boring cunt. Look at them having the time of their lives, and I'm stuck next to you, ya dry lunch."

Tommy is one of my tartan army brothers, Freddie being the other. We have travelled the world together and I love them like real brothers. But that doesn't mean we have to be nice to each other.

"Fuck off, junkie." He pushes my face half-heartedly away and goes back to sleep. His breath is like that of a thousand camels, so I let him be. To be honest, I want to join him. I have only been drinking this long to keep the impending hangover at bay. I put on my sunglasses and drift off into a fitful, uncomfortable sleep.

I check us into our accommodation, and everyone is raging with me. The first leg of the trip in Brazil was left to me to book all our hotels. We are on a budget; well, I am. I am still working in a shitty IT job. The rest of them are well into successful careers, mostly in ridiculously overpaid North Sea oil jobs. So catering to my budget and not theirs, I found a really good-looking backpacking hostel in the heart of Sao Paulo. Walking distance from the downtown nightlife. It is a fucking dive.

We struggled to find it, as the entrance is jammed between a fruit grocer and a butcher's. The smell of offal, the stale BO of the woman checking us in and the smog of the city combine to make an overpowering, noxious smell on entry. There is a sheen of grime on everything that could not be attributed to the humidity. I can feel six pairs of eyes boring into the back of my head as we were all checked into the same big room. Four sets of rickety metal bunkbeds are presented in front of us that are not fit for Auschwitz.

The smelly woman who checked us in slams the door behind us, sealing me into my fate. The only stars on Tripadvisor this place is going to get are the ones above my head when this lot kick my cunt in. Thankfully, everyone's hangovers and jetlag overpower their disgust for our new humble abode, and we all crash out. I climb up into the top bunk, which sways and grinds with my featherweight frame, and pass out in my kilt.

I am awoken by an almighty skelp to my bare arse. The shock of if causes me to buck and crack my head on the low ceiling. A chorus of laughter fills the room. "Breakfast is served, Michael Palin." More laughter.

I jump out of bed and join the excited group, my penance for our hovel over. Mike has served us up a continental treat. He is short, sharp witted and full of blunt comments. He is a renowned shagger and he lets you know it, full of life and constantly trying to compensate for I don't know what. He was ever the early riser and had been out wandering and had found a supermarket tucked away between two high-rise flats. Before me is a mix of what looks like soggy croissants, blocks of cheese, vodka and beer. Hair of the dog it is.

It is match day anyway, the opening match of the World Cup 2014. Scotland hadn't qualified as usual, but we had all opened a joint bank account at the start of the qualification period, back when we still had hopes and dreams of making it. Typical Scotland. Being a fan of the Scotland national team is what Irvin was talking about: "It's shite being Scottish." We haven't qualified for a major tournament since France '98. There must be something in our genes to continue to support them, something akin to what makes mothers forget the agony of childbirth and want additional children. A qualifying campaign would begin with a deluded confidence and hysteria that would slowly erode to well-worn disappointment. We had saved too much by the time it was mathematically impossible for us to not qualify, so we all thought, fuck it, and went anyway.

Once our nutritious breakfast is eaten, we ask smelly ogre to book us a taxi to the fan zone. The one thing I did get right about my booking was that it is only a ten-minute taxi ride, a stone's throw away in this sprawling metropolis of Sao Paulo. We arrive at what can only be described as a holding pen for Guantanamo Bay. Everyone is being thoroughly frisked for weapons on entry.

We had been warned beforehand that Sao Paulo is notorious for gun crime, and as tourists we would be targeted for kidnapping. Walking up to the security check, it is always funny to see the confusion on people's faces when tasked with frisking a drunk Scot in a kilt. Do they pat down our bare legs? Can they check up our kilt? Is our sporran a bag? The majority of the time our arms are patted down and we are waved through. This is what happens this time, and I get into the fan zone safely, with my sporran hiding a hipflask full of rusty nail (two parts single malt, one-part Drambuie, burns like hell).

It is ten in the morning, and the temperature is already thirty-eight degrees, a stifling, humid heat that soaks our clothes and makes our kilts three times as heavy. The sun is hidden behind the smog of the city, but its presence is always known. The fan zone is already close to capacity, with representatives from all the qualifying nations and now from one left behind. As usual, we are a spectacle for all the other fans, buying us drinks, wanting to know why we are here, asking for photos or telling us they hate the English as much as us. (We don't hate the English, just love the rivalry. Well, we hate their media. And their yobs.)

With a group of Argentinians, through broken English and us doing our best accents in raised voices, we discuss the heroics of Maradonna and his hand of God. Travelling all over the globe supporting Scotland, it seems to me the British are the most ignorant in the world. We go to countries, and it is expected of us that everyone will speak English, and we are generally right. Everywhere we go, people will speak their own language and English either fluently or at least broken. Why are we the only country that refuses to learn a second language? Still living in the past glory of the British empire where we once enslaved half the world.

We meet a local, who stands and drinks with us for a few hours. He speaks good English and is going to the match on his own. He offers to be our guide out to the stadium for the opening game. We get a minibus taxi to take us all out to the stadium. After ten minutes in the taxi, the skyscrapers out of the window abruptly end and favelas appear, corrugated metal shanty huts climbing over the top of each other like drowning men frantically trying to escape the flood.

We drive past the aftermath of a riot. The militia police kneel on people's backs while they handcuff them, and barefoot children run around legions of mounted soldiers. Roberto explains that there have been riots that have descended into armed warfare between the population and the police. People are not happy about how much the corrupt government has spent trying to host the World Cup then the Olympics in quick succession, while eighty per cent of the population live in poverty. The extent of the poverty is apparent driving past the favelas.

The taxi drops us off over a mile from the stadium. It cannot take us any further due to the sea of bodies. Football is a religion in Brazil, and there is a pilgrimage of yellow in front of us.

Wearing a kilt in a foreign country makes you an instant celebrity. People point and stare as you walk past; you are asked to pose for photos; women hang off you like jewellery; old men pull you aside to recount war stories and men who, without you wearing your kilt amour would stab you for your pocket change, buy you drinks at the bar. As the English are known for starting fights and throwing plastic lawn chairs at policemen, the Scots are known for getting pished and having a good time. A kilt in a foreign land is like raising the international white flag. I choose to raise it as pirate flag and corrupt any locals silly enough to fall under its glamour.

I pose for photos with a short, dark-haired Brazilian girl with her chest hanging out. As thanks, she hugs me and sticks her tongue in my mouth. I can taste the alcohol on her breath, and she offers me a drink of some horrible concoction out of her purse, which I can taste my hangover from already. She slips her arm round my waist and without so much as exchanging names, we march towards the stadium. I feel a sharp toe volley me up the arse, then Freddie shouts, "I hope you told her you have crabs!" Jealous cunt.

We arrive at a large market square at the foot of the stadium, a towering concrete monster which is still unable to shelter us from the baking sun directly overhead. I do not register the smell of garbage in the area until I notice its absence. The marketplace smells of fresh bread, spices and warmth. The stalls must have been whisked away last minute to make room for this mini carnival before us. There is music blaring out from the stadium's speakers; people are kicking footballs about the crowd. Sexy, exotic girls are dancing in groups, and everyone seems to have a drink in their hand.

"Apologies, Andrew," I say to Muncle. Not an hour earlier I had called him a fat wank for dragging us out to the stadium without tickets just for the atmosphere. We are treated like kings, and people queue up to get a photo or give a drink to the drunk Scots. Football is love and unity. Whenever I hear of a terrorist attack or a county invading another, I think back to this moment. Monsters try to divide us, but football can unite us. It proves we are one living breathing organism.

Hours slip by and I get drunker and drunker. The new love of my life has slipped off into the haze, and at some point, I notice the throng of people disappearing into the stadium.

I begin to feel a white-hot pain growing behind my eyes. I shake it off as too much drink, and a group of locals lead us to a small bar where we can watch the opening game and get a drink in the shade. The urgent feeling, I get when I'm on the drink to get as drunk as possible and locate every drug within a five-mile radius has disappeared by half-time. It has been replaced by this headache I cannot shake. It's not the drink or a pre-emptive hangover, so I mumble something to Tommy about getting a taxi home.

The heat as I walk out of the air-conditioned bar hits me like a hammer. I still have some wits about me to know I have the beginnings of sunstroke. This is on top of dehydration and exhaustion from days of alcohol binges. I feel like a zombie staggering down the streets looking for a taxi. The kilt glamour had worn off due to my shambling, drunken appearance, so people now cross the street to avoid me. I can barely lift my eyes to see where I am going. Ten minutes of wandering aimlessly, forgetting I am even looking for a taxi, I look up and my heart drops. I have somehow drunkenly wandered into a favela. I sober up instantly. Spinning in a circle, all I can see is mud, wooden huts with iron roofs and a sea of eyes staring at me.

A group of black men are watching me from across the street. There are about five of them, in their mid-twenties, all were wearing Brazil tops and all looking dangerous. I lock eyes with one of the guys in the middle, and time seems to freeze. The group begins marching towards me. This is it, I think. Knifed in a favela, never to be found. A laugh escapes my lips at the thought of me lying bleeding on the ground, my kilt thrown up and my dick hanging out. A last fuck you to my attackers. The lead guy in the mob looks confused by my laugh, and his menacing looks soften. He extends his hand to me to shake and says, "You lost, friend?" I shake his hand and prepare myself for the punch. An old cunt's trick, to go to shake someone's hand, hold on tight then punch them as hard as you can with your other hand. No punch comes.

"Can we have a photo with you, friend?"

The kilt strikes again. I take several photos with the group, one on everyone's phone. In broken English, they tell me they love the Scots, hate the English and are amazed at how lost I've got. I am two miles from the stadium! Some march I must have had on. The guys could not have been nicer. Instead of the quick death in the gutter I was expecting, they lead me through the

66

narrow, winding streets of the favela, flag me down a taxi and make sure I am not ripped off with the price. Next thing I know, I am being shaken awake by my taxi driver outside our hovel. I stagger inside and flop on the metal bunkbed, nearly causing it to collapse. Unconsciousness claims me.

I sleep for sixteen hours and wake up feeling brand new. Today, I am determined to find coke. So close to Columbia, it must be ten times purer than the pish I would snort at home. In Scotland, you would be lucky to get ching that is sixty per cent pure. Changing so many hands on its route from Columbia to my nose means it is cut at every stop on its way for the greedy cunts to increase their profits. I had read that I should expect the coke to be upwards of ninety per cent here and to tone down my lines.

Would I fuck. Sidney Devins like albino's eyebrows are my plan for the day. If in a strange country with no dealer, the best thing to do to find drugs is to find a whore first, or failing that a strip club.

Some lengths I have gone to following this plan. I took my family to Disneyland Florida one year and met up with a friend and his family. We were granted a rare night of freedom from sunburnt, gurny kids to go have a pint and watch a Rangers game. The night progressed and before I knew it, I was texting hookers then having to send them dick pics from the pub toilet to prove I wasn't a cop. All 'cos we wanted coke. I got it in the end, but it was a surreal sequence of events. My mate didn't even help me take the photo or thank me once the coke arrived, the ungrateful bastard.

It is late afternoon by the time I get up and shower. The only other person who is up and not in their own personal hangover hell is Gaz. Gaz is a tall, heavy-set boy with soft features, a massive head and insane strength. Trying to shove him off the ball at football is like running into a brick wall. Cunt could stick a thumb up his arse and hold himself at arm's length.

Gaz has always been a funny shifty cunt. When Dave and Carly bought a house, Gaz moved into their old flat. I was drinking in the station pub with Pete (the dealer I met at T in the Park, who was shovelling ching up my nose) and Gaz was texting, asking for ching. He was in Inverness and said to meet him in his flat in an hour. I convinced Pete that I knew how to climb up a lamppost and get into a loose window in the flat. I had to do it several times when Dave lived there, as he always lost his keys. Our plan was to break in then scare Gaz shitless when he got home.

I shimmied up the lamppost and squeezed into the loose window then let Pete in the door. We waited and waited for Gaz to arrive, and the longer we waited, the more drugs we sniffed off his coffee table. He took so long we ended up Snap-chatting him, blowing our cover by sending pics of us in his flat taking lines. Gaz thought it was hilarious but thought it would be even more hilarious to phone the police.

Fucking cops showed up ten minutes later, chapping on the door, shouting in that they had the place surrounded. I've never seen a cunt of Pete's size move with such speed. He was a blur, dashing to the toilet and emptying every pocket into the bowl. He was pulling bags from every place imaginable and flushing furiously. Cops were still banging on the door when Pete grabbed me.

"I'm just outta jail; I'm no going back. If it comes to it, you're my fucking hostage."

Not again, I thought.

He was crawling along the floors like he was in a fox hole. "Fucking get down, you cunt, or I'll put you down."

68

I lay down on the floor with him, when Gaz phoned us in howls of laughter. "No funny now, is it, ya mongos."

"Gaz, this is no joke now. Pete is getting nam flashbacks. Phone the cops an tell them it was a mistake."

"Okay Junkie, see ya soon, haha."

The cops had stopped banging, but I knew they were watching the flat. We couldn't leave. Then I got a text from Gaz saying he had phoned them and said he locked us in by accident, just answer the door. I told Pete this.

"If you do this, you better do it right, you cunt, 'cos if they come in here, I won't leave easy."

Okay, okay. I took off my t-shirt, tussled my hair, and when the police banged on the door again five minutes later, I answered.

"What's going on officer? I've just woken up."

"We had a report of a break in, sir. Is it just you in the house?"

"Yes officer. I fell asleep, and everyone that was here fucked off and left me," I replied, all confused. Selling sand to the Arabs once again.

"Okay, sir, call us if you need us."

"Gaz's fucking a dead man when he gets here," Pete growled. Fuck sake, man. Drama twenty-four seven.

He didn't kill Gaz, 'cos Gaz arrived laughing his ass off and was carrying a wad of cash and a bag of drugs. The flushed contents of Pete's pockets were paid for, and the three of us went to work on Gaz's bag. Have to stay on your toes with Gaz. But on reflection, I did break into his flat. Fucking blinkers on, me.

We jump in a taxi, and through the taxi driver's broken English and Gaz's sign language of his cupping a large set of breasts, we are dropped off outside a pink flashing neon sign of a girl swinging round a pole. When we enter, we are an instant novelty to the girls and also a meal ticket.

Gaz is a flashy cunt, buying champagne and drinks for us all. A girl is leering over me, wanting me to buy a dance. Her make-up is running, and a druggie can spot a druggie. I know she is on something. Her grinding on my lap suggests there is more on the menu than a dance. To our luck and detriment, there are apartments next to the strip club, rented by the hour. Negotiating our way out of the strip club with two girls in tow is a mission. Gaz is already playing up to his chosen companion.

"I love you, baby, you buy champagne."

"Away and take your face for a shite," he says to her with a smile on his face.

"Gaz, I'm pretty sure she kens what you're saying, ya prick," I laugh at him. But she doesn't, or if she does, she holds a good poker face. Gaz buys the champagne anyway like she knew he would. We are stupid foreigners and so drunk and gullible that we would pounce on any suggestion. I had to pay to take the girl away, then the bouncer hit me with a handbag charge.

"What the fuck is this? Paying for her to take her handbag?" I was quietly told by the girl that her handbag had the condoms in it, as she slipped her hand up my kilt. I was not to be dissuaded.

"What's next? You gonna hit me with a charge to get both of her fake tits out the club as well?"

Gaz threw money at the bouncer, grabbed me by the scruff of the neck and dragged me across the balcony into our new home for the hour.

The girl I was with was beautiful, but I have forgotten her face. She gave me a fake stripper name, crystal chandelier or something equally stripperish but as the night progressed she told me her real name was Jodie. All we did was take drugs together for an hour and talk shite. She was more well-read than my which I found more attractive than her looks, showing you can't judge a book by its cover Taking line after line on the glass table which seemed to be placed there just for this reason, it became apparent she was just looking for a kick like me, in the only profession she could. The oldest job in the world. Even though I can't remember her face, I still remember the connection we shared. Two lost souls looking for something but with no idea what it was or how to find it. Ghosts passing in the night.

Drunk, high, dazed and looking for more kicks than life had to offer, the four of us cram into her tiny Beetle car, champagne in hand and small mirror from Gaz's twenty-four hour wife's handbag to sniff ching, we set off into the night, looking for adventure and more drugs.

I can't imagine being any other way than this. Wherever I go, I am drawn to the seedy underworld. The dingy bars with the shady men going about their shady business. Where outlawed pleasures can be found, but violence is just a wrong word away. Where rules are scoffed at and those who abide by them shunned. This is where I belong. Risking my life by being driven around a strange country by a couple of drunk hookers looking for drugs. Thrills on top of thrills on top of thrills. Shadows and spice and all things nice. Gaz has his head out the window like a big, retarded Alsatian. The Joker in *The Dark Knight*.

Gaz and I are in back seat having the time of our lives, not a care in the world. The whores take a turn off the main strip and drive down into an unlit underground carpark. Our hearts drop. More thoughts of my death flash into my head. Not mugged in a favela this time but shot in a carpark, sporran stolen, whores laughing at our idiocy. The girls have gone silent and are typing furiously on their phones.

An ominous silence stretches in the car. Two guys appear from the shadows and approach from opposite sides. One strides up to me. Wiry, sharp and rodent-like, his eyes gleam in the dark. "Scottish?"

"Yes, my friend," I say in the stupid accent that comes out of me when speaking to anyone foreign.

"Ahh, we love the Scottish. I will get the best coke for you, straight from Columbia." Relief floods me. No dark death once again but a slower one, bled out line by line. More money thrown out the window and the rest of the night speeding past in a blur of high-rise flats viewed from a moving car and a spinning head.

I awake the next day naked in my rickety army cot with a hell of a hangover. The bag of coke is lying next to me. A rubber balloon, nearly empty, with residue of gummy coke inside. Fuck knows how we were managing to snort it. There is something else growing inside me. Part of the hangover but not. A sense of impending doom. I am scared, so I go back to sleep.

I am shaken awake several hours later by Muncle. "Mon, that's our time up in Motel Six, thank fuck."

I had only booked the first three nights of our stay in Sao Paulo; my uncle had booked the next five nights. He is minted and a flashy cunt, so I am looking forward to our new digs. Several years before, we arrived in Jacksonville, USA, for a Scotland game, and he had arranged for us to be picked up in a white Hummer limo. Like I said, flash cunt. Confused and excitable Yanks were lining up for autographs as we walked through the airport in our kilts and then waited for the Hummer. They thought we were the national team. Like kilt is everyday dress in Scotland, and my fifty-year-old grey dad is fit to play international football. God bless the Yanks.

There is honestly no place like America. My wife and I did

a bit of travelling after a family holiday at Disneyland. We went down to Miami then flew to LA, up to Vegas, to New York then home. Proper tourists. Got a carry-out and got drunk on the beach in Miami, because my wife was only twenty at the time. I was drawn to the Whisky Ago Go and the Viper Club where River Phoenix overdosed, in LA.

In Vegas, my wife got drunk in the hotel room and passed out, so I played Blackjack at the five dollar table all night. Word spread round the pit that Bin Laden had been killed. Drunk Yanks were cheering and throwing chips in the air, with tight Scottish me snatching them out of the air before they hit the ground. Tight as two coats of paint, I tell ya. Lastly, walking around New York with our heads tilted up constantly. I love the US of A and I love the Yanks.

On a trip to Jacksonville with the tartan army, a tropical storm warning was in effect, with all the shops and bars shut and windows boarded up. The strip club was open though, well, more a brothel. My mate got a lap dance, which ended with her pulling the kilt up and fucking him for a few dollars more. Soon as I found out, I grabbed her for a dance then yelled across the room, "I'm away to stir yer porridge, pal," to my dad's shame. The land of the free.

We spend maybe an hour in the taxi, flitting to our new hotel, but due to the traffic probably only move five miles through the city. We arrive at a shiny white high-rise Hilton Hotel. I am sharing my new room with Jack, a fat, quick-witted man, who always has an acute perspective on life and a scathing comment for anyone who does not fit this view. Our room is on the fifty-fourth floor. It is a wide, open-plan room with a massive TV and a dining table full of fruit for our arrival. The most striking feature though is a wide sliding door that opens onto a small balcony. The view of the city is less than impressive, just identical high-rise flats as far as you can see, and smog. Like soldiers standing to attention in the mist. I stand out on the balcony and look over the chest-high wall. Strange, no railing, I think. Then it hits me: the clawing, grating nervousness I have been feeling all day manifests into a voice in my head I have never heard before, my own, but not.

"Jump, climb over and jump!" The feeling of impending doom comes back and grips me tight. My whole body breaks out in shivers, and my breath catches in my bone-dry throat. Nausea rips through me and I find myself leaning further and further over the wall, smiling. My feet are off the ground, with all my weight on my chest on the wall. I am lying horizontal, ready to tip over, then I snap out of my trance.

The pull of the abyss recedes, and the voice telling me to jump becomes a whisper. My feet touch the ground, and I slam the balcony door shut. Jack finds me in the room, sitting with my head in my hands. I am shaking and sweat is pishing off me. My fight-or-flight response has always been skewed. Flight is never chosen, and when the response kicked in on the balcony, my instinct was to fight the danger of falling. Go head-first into the concrete fifty-four stories below with a grin on my face. I have never felt like this before in my life. A death wish I had never acknowledged manifested in the form of a soulless voice. I am terrified, scared to even look at the balcony. I can feel the call, the pull of it, even sitting with my eyes shut. We are due to stay in this hotel for five nights before flying to Rio de Janerio. Five nights of torture, of resisting the urge to throw myself off, ignoring a voice and feeling that was so insistent now it has escaped from subconscious to conscious thought. I get a flight home from Brazil the next day.

Persistence of Memory

I snapped back to reality. Pain dominated my consciousness. I could only see out of one eye, with the other completely swollen shut. Blood ran in sheets down my face, and a terror had settled over me like a cold shroud. Existential dread, pure Lovecraftian horror. Death had a grip of me, and my lifetime of toying with it felt utterly idiotic now I knew what I was playing with. All hope had fled, and I wanted to run with it. Pure terror is not a feeling. It is a knowing. I knew of all the evil in the world at that instant, knew of the unimaginable monsters we create of ourselves and the ones beyond this world we cannot even comprehend. My guts had been torn out and my breath ripped from throat. My mind was being flayed with the knowledge of death.

I squinted my working eye at my surroundings, and the stars had faded, withered trees had grown around me and melted clock faces hung off them like dead leaves, ready to be blown away on a death rattle. The fog was knee high, with the tendrils reaching nearly to my chest. When the drip of my blood met the fog, it hissed away as if burning up in a fire, even though the fog chilled my heart. Rand stood before me. He had grown in height, and his shadow leered over me. He seemed to be wearing jesters' clothes from the feudal era, and he was juggling dark stars. There was a hypnotic rhythm to the movements which dragged my gaze subconsciously away from his grin and his now needle-sharp teeth.

"Funny, isn't it. I never tire of eating the despair people

exhale when they realise death is all that and more. I don't even care your opinion on this memory and how much it fucked you up. Did I forget to mention the rules have changed? A paradigm shift. All of life is a game. It is rigged, so to have a hope of winning, you must cheat. And god loves a chancer. That's what you told yourself, isn't it, Marty? Unfortunately, this is far from the truth. Life is not a game, and god fucking hates a chancer. No more being spoon-fed memories – you must pick them now. Take your time; you are nearly all mine." Rand practically sang this to me, never breaking eye contact and never losing rhythm with the stars' graceful juggling. How he managed to talk with his long sharp teeth was all that I could think about.

"Ignore him," Bill said. "You still have a chance to save yourself."

Bill had shrunk and he looked frail. The stars were going out in his face, leaving him with a black shadow, outlines only visible as they sucked the light. His white clothes were stained in blood and ash, as he had been tending to me while my mind was in the past. "You must think, not follow your gut, as you have done all your life, but think! Think on the consequences of your actions; think on how you are perceived, not just how you perceive yourself. Think on the risks you have taken and what you risk to lose."

Thoughts seemed to slip through my grasp and I had to focus all my will to think coherently. All my previous transgressions and actions now disgusted me. I looked on my life in a different light. Drink and drugs had dominated my entire life. Weekends were the only time I was lucid, if being drunk and high counts as lucid. Weekdays I entered a catatonic state, a zombie going through the motions until I could come back to life again. My weekday life held in prison by the monster I turned into on the weekend, like a werewolf on a full moon.

My bravado and blasé attitude covering up for a deeply

76

insecure and broken boy. Overcompensating in the face of crippling shyness. Brave but stupid. Intelligent but a fucking idiot… I used to climb trees when I was young, a lot of them. On windy days I would climb to the very top of a tree, clinging to the thinnest branches that would support me and just feel the sway of the tree. I think this sums me up – looking for peace in danger. Solace in chaos. Skirting danger to quiet voices in my head I had not yet begun to acknowledge.

I survived like this for years, happy I thought. I never really had a direction but I was content with where I was heading. You can have all the tools in the world, but if you don't have the motivation to go with them then you are just a caveman sitting in the mud. I coasted through life, always living for the now, never tomorrow. Having faith in empiricism and that tomorrow would always provide fresh opportunities.

I held an almost disdain for money, letting it burn a hole in my pocket. These two facts are what restrained me from ever pursuing a career seriously. I went from job to job, location to location, once landing in Canada, teaching snowboarding for a season. Funnily enough, the town I stayed in was called Banff, named after the town an hour's drive from my home. This was just an extended season-long party. I lived in a hostel that had its own bar below the rooms, called the Cellar, and I spent every night for five months in there.

When I arrived, I was bundled into a room with a charismatic, innocent but willingly corruptible Londoner named Connor and an outgoing, sweet but also corruptible Aussie named Dan. Within a week, I knew I had made lifelong friends as we debauched our way around and the hostel and the slopes, throwing and crashing parties as we saw fit. On the final night of the season, we climbed a small mountain and got drunk and stoned looking at the stars. The Milky Way is a different animal when viewed intoxicated, surrounded by the Canadian Rockies.

Without a wisp of light pollution to dim the view, it was the first memory I got when I opened my eyes in this purgatory. Before it turned against me.

Connor, Dan and I spoke of our hopes and dreams while passing a bottle and a joint back and forth. We asked were we thought we would be in ten years' time. They were both so unsure of themselves, talking about possible jobs or careers. I stated for a fact I would be married with kids, because I knew that's exactly what I wanted. Money, jobs and possessions never held any value to me. Life has been good to me, as I got exactly what I wanted. A gorgeous wife and two amazing boys and a beautiful daughter. I never imagined though that the monkey paw would clench into a fist and I would be dead of an overdose in ten years.

When did the party stop? When did the casual drug taking, promiscuous lifestyle and disregard for my own safety become the ruling forces in my life? Not doors in my mind to walk through but the very foundation of my mind itself. I am ashamed of the strain my actions and disregard for consequences must have placed on my family. My poor, poor parents. They were never bad parents; I was just a bad son. Nature over nurture and all that. Or at least I hope. I like to think I am an individual and not just a moulded piece of clay. My soul is eternal and devoid of all stimuli would still have the same personality. Funny to think of a soul as having a personality.

My soul! The fog in my mind clears and I am pulled back from my ruminations to the dire situation I am in. I am so close to losing my soul to this demon masquerading as Rand. I think I know what tipped me into insanity. My eyes lock with Bill's. He nods his head, as he knows I have made a decision. I close my eyes again and fall into the mist.

SPHELL

I worked two jobs at SPL: the first was the hot, sweaty, dangerous manual labour we did to make carbon fibre; the second was the web of drug dealing I had set up with the two hundred-odd willing staff of SPL.

SPL produces carbon fibre. This is done by running a precursor in a continuous line from a box via a complicated series of rollers, through two massive ovens the size of a house, through two furnaces, then through a bath to wash it with ammonia. Then it is wound onto spools to be packed. This process is very labour intensive. The ovens run at over six hundred degrees and the furnaces at over eight hundred. Fires are common, and the offset of carbonising the precursor is HCN. This is hydrogen cyanide, used in World War One and world war two gas chambers It is hard, dangerous work, and the labour force is underpaid, under-appreciated and looked down on by management.

The hierarchy in SPL is unlike any other workplace and goes like this.

The Masons with their secret handshakes and folded letters. Winking eyes and wanking each other off in a circle like they are singing "Auld Lang Syne". A guy there who bought ching off me had more holidays than the queen and had a meteoric rise to team leader because he became the Grandmaster of the local lodge. Still didn't stop him buying my gear.

Below them are the army boys. If you are an ex-service man and turn up for an interview, then the job is yours. I have no problem with this. I have nothing but respect for people who put their lives at risk for others, but I would never volunteer for service myself. I'm a pacifist at heart and have no desire to kill a shepherd in another country just so someone can line their pockets from it. Veterans get preferential treatment at SGL due to the site manager being one himself. They get the easier jobs, they get the pick of overtime shifts and they get away with murder.

Then there are us: the peasants, the scum, the proles, the dossers.

So, we take drugs at work. A lot of drugs. I once started a shift and before my first break, from separate people I had been offered a line of morphine, tramadol, coke, dihydrocodeine, THC, vape and my bread and butter, goblins (pregabalin).

We worked hard, but in essence it was a boys' club. Twelve hours with your friends getting the craic, gambling and taking drugs. I looked forward to going to work. Every morning or afternoon, depending on what shift I was on, I would wake up, take a line of coke, neck a rake of goblins, then sort out what drugs and for whom I was bringing into work.

I would get my drugs on Telegram. It's an app similar to WhatsApp but more heavily encrypted. It is the new Silk Road, and once you have made the right connections and are added into the correct groups, it is heaven for a drug dealer. I could go onto Telegram and order goblins and coke at one p.m., and it would be delivered to my door in the post the next day. I have had more problems with orders from Amazon than I have had ordering drugs on Telegram. I was on this from its infancy when everyone migrated from the dark web. Most payments were in Bitcoin, but this slowly changed to accommodate banks as the user base grew.

My income skyrocketed and my addictions followed suit. At the height of dealing drugs at work, I was making over a grand a month. It's not exactly *Scarface* material, but a grand I didn't have to hide or justify going missing to my wife was huge. I should have spent it on my boys, but it went up my nose. I remember one roasting hot summer day; the lines were down and everyone had time on their hands. Twice I was sent on a forty-mile roundtrip in my boss's car to pick up more coke. Like I said, boys' club.

"You watch the line for me. I'm off to the penthouse."

"Fucking again? You will not have any gear left by tea, buster." Jason was a bald Jack the Lad, with a weathered face, in his mid-forties, though he looked in his sixties. Hard paper round for him.

I share a lift in to work with him, and in the twenty-minute drive in he manages to smoke ten fags. One is lit before the other one is out. We arrive to work with my car looking like a snow globe with all his ash floating about. A borderline alcoholic, I once picked him up for work steaming, and we walked into a shit show. Fires everywhere and we were running about trying to keep the line running. Jason was standing under a heated roller looking confused and talking shite to me while I tried to fix the line. "You have a clue what you're doing, Jason?"

"Do I fuck, son. I'm mortal!"

"You know you're burning your head on that heated roller?"

"Owww, ya, fuck, I didn't notice."

That's Jason in a nutshell – no noticing he is burning his heed 'cos he's drunk and talking shite to ya. He has a heart of gold but he is a chancer and loves a gossip. Queen of the SPL sewing circles is Jason, and SPL has some sewing circles, I tell ya.

It's like being back in school with the gossip flying about. There is always some cunt arguing with another and shady shit going on all over site. You could fart at one end of the site and by the time you got to the other, you had shit yourself.

"Just watch the line; my nose is hungry." The penthouse is a side room that feeds the water for the furnace deluge, and it is locked by a key code. Only the furnace ops have the code, but one gave it to me so I could turn it into a drug den. I would go in, lock the door, then take out the sheet of metal I had found and hidden in there for cutting up lines. Line and a fag in the SPL penthouse was a common occurrence on a twelve-hour shift.

"I was wondering when you would arrive."

"Oo ya fucker, I near shit myself" Josh was sitting in the penthouse, smoking in the dark like some James Bond villain.

Ah, Josh. What to say about him? Love of my narcotic life; Thelma to my Louise. He is the third person in my car share to work, and us meeting was like two hurricanes colliding, the perfect storm He is a charismatic man, in his middle age, with long hair and a beard. Good-looking in the right light and like me he is bipolar. For every drug or trick he taught me, I taught him one in return. We took so many drugs together we ended up like women who spend so long in each other's company that their menstrual cycles sync up – our manic-depressive cycles synced. When we were both depressed, we sucked each other into our void. When we were manic, we bounced off the walls together, planning to take over the world. Almost a folie a deux. Madness of two. Or just two fucking idiots. Our first night out together, we were out of our faces on a manic swing he made a request I will never forget

"Clink shovels with me."

"Eh? What you on about?"

"You know, when two guys are digging a hole and they accidentally clink shovels, they share a look with each other, then just get on wi the job. Let's double team a whore and do that wi our knobs."

I fell on the floor laughing and told him to go find his own hole to dig. Drugs were my only vice now.

Together we started the goblin revolution in work. We were taking upwards of fourteen 300 mg tablets a shift. This was funded by me shifting goblins to every other worker on site.

Josh got dihydrocodeine on script and we ate them like sweeties. One time when we were struggling, we set up a cold-water filtration system in the penthouse to filter out the paracetamol from co-codamol to leave us with the sweet codeine. You can only take 800 mg of paracetamol a day before your liver starts to shut down, and we were skirting this daily. A perfect storm.

That's the two rockets in my car share. The drive into work with the three of us is just a blizzard of drugs to get as high as possible before we endure twelve hours of exhausting, back breaking shite.

I exited the penthouse, and Jason was looking all flustered. "Theo was down looking for you, son. He was raging you weren't here."

Theo is a short, bald wee cunt with a chip on his shoulder and a Napoleon complex. He has almost baby-like features which match the temper tantrums he throws. He is also our team leader and had a vendetta against me. I actually liked him and knew he could be coerced into my madness. Once, we went on a work day out to the horse races in Perth. He got drunk on the bus on the way down and I managed to convince him to let me take a line of coke off his bald head.

I dunno if that says more about how I bring out the worst in people or that his angry personality is just a façade.

In work he hated me, because he could never get a rise out

83

of me. No matter how mental he went or how much venom he spat my way, I would just smile at him. This seemed to get under his skin more than me dodging work and taking drugs. Well, he could never prove I was taking drugs at work, but he had his suspicions. Most of the other boys crawled up his arse, and this got under my skin just as much as me smiling at him got under his. Fucking sycophants everywhere.

Theo rounded the corner with steam pissing out of his ears. He was bright red, and it made his head looked like a slapped arse. "Where the fuck were you?"

"I was down helping them fight that fire."

"You couldn't fight sleep, you cunt. You are like Houdini with your disappearing."

"Away, mun. You love a magician, always disappearing with a poof." My humour was lost on him, and he looked fit for a stroke.

"If I catch you away from the line again, I'll pull you up to the office, you wanker."

I was always threatened with being pulled up to the office. A rift had opened up between the blue-collar workforce and the white-collar office staff. The terrible working conditions, the disdain and lack of respect from management had tempers at boiling point. The management seemed to think we should just suck it up and get on with it. That our complaining about dangerous working conditions and shite pay was just pure ungratefulness. It was almost like a feudal system, with the kings and lords presiding over us peasants.

The only cunt Theo hated in SPL more than me was Stan. Stan would take the abuse Theo threw his way to heart more than me, and it ended up being constituted as bullying. Stan was a kid at heart, and it near broke him.

Stan came into work one night boasting about how his friend grew magic mushrooms and he could get me capsules full of them anytime I wanted. This being the middle of July, ten months after mushy season, and Stan being a notorious liar, I decided to call his bluff.

Stan was sound as fuck, a man-child in stature and maturity. He was short and wiry, with muscles built from long hours on his BMX and skateboard. He was covered in tattoos, and even though he knew we were right, had a hatred for anyone caught mocking his childlike obsessions. One night, he was assigned the task of cleaning the floors with a drive-on floor washer. I snuck up and pinned a yellow triangle on the back, declaring a child on board. He chased me round site with a mop handle when he discovered why everyone was laughing at him as he drove past all night.

For once, he wasn't talking shite and turned up the next night with two capsules for me to test. The following night was my weekend off, and I had planned a sesh with Dave and Carly. As usual, Dave and I ended up on the coke. Carly hated it in the house, so we kept sneaking out to his shed to do lines. Two in the morning rolled around. Carly had gone to bed, and Dave and I just stayed in the shed singing loudly to tunes played on our phones to no audience but the garden tools.

Suddenly, Dave's phone switched from playing The View to a buzzing call with Carly's picture on the screen, already looking angry in my coked-out head. I started getting ready to leave before he even answered and resigned myself to the long walk home. Two minutes into the walk home while rooting through my pockets for a fag, my fingers closed around the mushy caps. Fuck it, I thought, which has been my lifelong mantra and the cause of many of my problems. Down the hatch dry. I have always had an uncanny knack for swallowing pills with no water. I've done eight 300 mg goblins in one gulp before.

It's not a long walk from Dave's to mine, but ten minutes later, as I was stabbing the door with my keys, trying to unlock it drunk in the dark (put hair round it and I would get it first time, Andy used to say), I started to feel the effects. I could physically feel the starlight on my back. Turning round was like looking into the heart of the cosmos. I have always been scared off psychedelics due to the horror stories of bad trips. I dread experiencing one due to the glimpses of the darkness inside of me that I have already experienced. This trip made me question it all: not just my trepidation, but my very existence. Why did I trudge through my dreary life just barely feeling normal, fighting for every glimmer of happiness when this was waiting for me? Maturity for me though is realising I'm not mentally stable enough to cope with regular psychedelics any more.

But I felt a oneness with everything, complete bliss that I have only ever experienced once before in my life. A time that shaped everything that was to follow, but we will get to that later.

My keys dropped from my hand and I put my back to the door and slid down to sit and stare at the stars. I tried not to blink for fear of losing this feeling. I travelled millions of light years to a dying star and swam in its supernova. Did backstroke through primordial togetherness. Felt affinity to each and every atom in the universe, then slowly the tug of my flesh pulled me back along the last light to be emitted from this star, and I returned to my body. I was hungover, on a comedown, freezing with a runny coke nose and under a cloud of depression from what I had just lost. The afterlife I hope for. I put my keys in the door first try and tried to sneak in without waking my wife. I slept like a baby.

My only other experience with mushrooms was when I was

a teenager. Me and Andrew, a big blockhead of a boy, who like me had a dangerously curious appetite. His head was shaped like a cinder block and was just as thick to match. He always wore a pleased look on his face like a puppy which had just returned a stick.

Back when we were all still using 56k dial-up, Andrew introduced me to the dark web. We experimented by ordering ten quid's worth of hash on the Silk Road with bitcoin that if used now would be worth twenty-odd grand.

This knowledge doesn't bother me at all.

We also found out where to find magic mushrooms and how to correctly spot them. There was a horse field behind my mum's house, so armed with our new knowledge, we managed to fill a plastic shopping bag full of Liberty caps within five minutes. A goldmine of a field. I dried them out under my bed in a pizza box and two days later we went to town. Stupid teenagers with no clue how to take them or how much to take, we just started munching the lot, stalks and all. We scoffed the whole pickings like a box of chips then jumped on the 25x bus to take us to a disco in Tain. Tain Town Hall was the central meeting point for all the surrounding towns on a Friday night.

New girls to try it on with but more often than not in our case, new guys to piss off. All the hard cunts from every town went here looking for trouble and poor innocent me, who was only looking for a good time, tended to end up with a sore face.

Not the most relaxed environment to have your first trip in.

It started to hit us on the bus. Frank was trying to convince me to buy eccies off him. The last ones he sold me were shite, so I was weighing up the options in my head of buying dud pills compared to him head-butting me and taking my money anyway. My hand was in my pocket, ready to take the lesser of two evils, when I found something utterly hilarious with my shoe.

"What the fuck are you laughing it?"

"Look at my shoe, Frank, just look at it," I blurted out. My shoe was now off and I was waving it in his face. "Fucking hell, touch it; look at it, then touch it."

Tears were streaming down my face with laughter and Frank was switching from mild annoyance to outright rage.

"Fuck's wrong with this cunt? He taking the piss?"

Andrew, who was sitting next to me, answered and had not yet quite got the joke.

"We've taken a heap of mushie, but I think he's putting it on."

Franks's tone changed and he started laughing, which only made me worse. Nothing then existed to me apart from my shoe.

Frank decided there were easier people to rip off who were less hassle and moved on, shaking his head.

He had once sold Andrew and me two eccies each. We were in the back of his car, and out of habit we both double-dunted them there and then. He started to freak out, saying they were super strong and we were gonna die. He didn't give a fuck about us; he just didn't want to be fingered as the cunt who sold the two corpses drugs. He made us stay in his car all night while he went about his business. At one point, when we were completely melted, me and Andrew had a competition of who could punch themselves in the face the hardest. We both lost. Shortly after, once he was convinced, we weren't going to go ten toes up, Frank dumped us at my house. Yes, there were definitely customers who were less hassle on that bus.

Interlude

August

Guilt is a constant companion these days. I have put Jaz through so much and still she stands by me. Why I don't know. I feel guilty for giving in to the voices; I feel guilty for all the drugs I chose over my family; I feel guilty for all the times I cheated on my wife; I feel guilty for wallowing in my own self-pity, but most of all I feel guilty for not being content with what I have. I have everything I ever wanted. A good job, a stunning wife and three amazing kids, yet it is not enough. I am sad all the time and still have a hole inside me. I feel guilty because this could all happen again. I don't know what this yearning inside me wants. I want it all to stop so I can just appreciate what I have. If not, I want to set my body on fire so I can be free.

The NHS has a failed me big style I think. Pre-Covid, I was coping, then isolation took over. I was cut off from all support that kept the wolves from the door. It's not really the NHS's fault. The NHS is a miracle of socialism. If *Breaking Bad* were set in the UK, Walter White would have gone to the doctor's, been told he had cancer, then got treatment from the NHS without needing to create a drug empire to pay for his medical bills. End of story. I failed myself. I am not a nice person to be around on my dark days, and during lockdown it was just me, myself and I squabbling in my own head. My psychiatrists, when I do hear from them, do nothing but nod at the horrors I try to explain are in my head. They sit in their ivory tower telling me it's all drug-related.

"Drugs are bad, Mr Douglas, but here are three prescriptions for you to take daily. Oh, by the way, keep us informed if you feel any side-effects. One tablet may cause organ failure and the other skin necrosis, and there may be additional side-effects, as we can't be sure how they will interact with each other."

"What, you mean like leprosy? Oh aye, cheers for that, Doc. Once I have got a necrotic grip, I won't be able to dial your number due to organ failure and my skin sliding off my hands."

The past ten years of my life have been doctors throwing tablets at me to see what would stick. Side-effects to side-effects, and each tablet normally ticks the box of turning me into a fat cunt. Only coke kept me thin: now it's gone, and my appetite is never satisfied. The funny thing is, the only prescription I have ever been given that even remotely helped me was gobblins. If only they weren't so moreish.

The life of an addict is not something you jump into. No single decision to chain a monkey to your back. Family on one scale and drugs and crime on another. Baby steps are taken, unconscious decisions glossed over as common sense in your mind. These small decisions lead to more, and before you know it, all the dominoes are falling, and you are left with a mess on the floor. Like a frog will sit in a frying pan with the heat slowly turning up till he is boiled alive. This is how junkies are created. Not born but peeled away to the core. And the line between darkness and light is so very thin.

Introspection is a wonderful thing and I have had a lot of time to do it these days. I can see my faults, the cracks and flaws. I can look deeper and see the catalysts for these character traits. My environment, upbringing, people I hung about with, decisions I made, wins and losses. But if I look deeper, something stares back, and it terrifies me. It was born with me; it waged war on me from my first breath and it will die with me. I can't run from it, and I now know I can't hide from it. Trying to kill it with narcotics did not work, and trying to kill myself with narcotics, dying a martyr, did not work either, as it rose from the dead with me. My own personal demon. If only this was *His Dark Materials* and my "daemon" was manifest so I could choke the life out of it.

Cocaine has found a way to blanket our society like a fresh fall of snow. Everyone does it, and everyone talks about it. No cunt can go for a few pints without phoning their dealer for a few grams. It is a nice, clean drug and seen as social as alcohol now. But every drug is dirty if you do it enough, and I had found a way to do cocaine filthy.

There is an art to properly cooking and inhaling crack. So much so that I am in a Reddit page online called "crack connoisseurs". Once you get the cooking down, and I had that to a T, you have to inhale it properly. You need to have the correct equipment first. A glass pipe is best, as it heats up and cools down quickly. Best for me sneaking an inhale in my bathroom. Then you need a good element to heat so that the crack will stick to and melt to the gas that is cocaine's base form. Copper is best: crack clings to it for dear life.

Heat up your rock slowly, never letting the flame touch. The crack will then melt and stick to the copper. This way, you don't burn the rock and waste any. Once it is melted to the copper, this is where you blast it with heat. Then inhale the sickly-sweet gas. Inhale till your lungs are fit to burst and hold your breath. Hold that crack in like it's a lover's embrace. Your head will spin and your bell will ring.

Can you tell I have slipped off the wagon again? It wasn't even my fault. The driver realised I didn't have a ticket and kicked me off.

YOU HAVE NOTHING TO LOSE
BUT YOUR CHAINS

I knew my time at SGL was coming to an end. It had been building up for months.

My drug-taking was at an all-time high; my dealing was attracting the attention of staff and my attendance was erratic. On top of it all, I had managed to con my way into becoming the union rep. We were in the middle of pay negotiations and I was throwing a spanner in the works at every opportunity. The last meeting I was in involved the head of SPL in Scotland, the head of our union, the head of the Scottish health and safety executive and me with a runny nose from taking too much ching before the meeting. Talking shite at a hundred miles an hour.

I had put a huge target on my back and I didn't care. Work was a game to me now. My mind was slowly slipping, with my addictions tightening their grip. I only went to work to see my customers and then spent all my time there antagonising management, thinking I was fighting the oppression of our working class. Delusions of being a revolutionary when in reality, I was just a druggie making waves in a sinking ship.

My final night at SPL was a culmination of all the drugs, my psychosis and the months of me ratteling cages and shaking trees with management.

The shift leader was strutting about, barking orders at cunts who were already breaking their backs for him. He was a wank. Proper Tory bell end who wore a golf cardigan to work in a sweltering hot factory. He had the biggest head on site, full of self-importance and arrogance. The dimensions of his head matched his ego. Head like a sniper's dream, large and bulbous. I was giving Calvin, a skinny, young lad, a lift in for the set, and he had the Saturday night off. When the shift leader strutted past us, not meeting my eyes as a pitiful sign of disrespect, I decided to poke the bear.

"Fancy giving me the Sat off as well pal, so me a Calvin can go on the drink together?"

This was at the height of Covid, and no one was supposed to be socialising together out of work. Redundant, seeing as we spent twelve hours a day climbing over each other, fighting wraps and fires. SPL's policy during Covid was negligent to the extreme, and me fighting them for the union was partly how I pissed off management.

They claimed we were essential workforce and carbon was needed to make medical equipment. A complete lie, which I took umbrage to. In a drug-fuelled psychosis, I began to spread propaganda, going as far as contacting a local councillor, who then in turn got an article in the local paper published about SPL. One quote was used from an anonymous source that SPL are in no way essential workforce and the only medical equipment their carbon is used in is in prosthetic legs. Fuck knows where I pulled that from; I must have been on a drug binge and watching *Pirates of the Caribbean*.

Anyway, he fuckin' exploded Greta Thunberg style "How dare you, how dare you put me and this whole plant at risk. Well, the rave the pair of you are planning is no happening. Calvin, your holiday is cancelled." And off he fucked without me even getting to tell him I was joking.

If he was in a rage it paled in comparison to mine now. The

poor cunt Calvin had his holiday cancelled on the whim of a fucking dick who was just doing it to spite me. The notion that it was my fault for winding him up in the first place never crossed my mind. I left where I was working and set out to find him. I confronted him in the shift leader's office and tried to be as diplomatic as possible.

" I think you got the wrong end of the stick there. I was only joking, and I never really wanted a holiday. I was only trying to bridge the animosity between us by extending an olive branch via humour." Trying to speak with plums in my mouth like I imagine his pals do while burning fifty pound notes in front of the homeless, but he was having none of it.

"It's boys like you who are going to get this place shut down. I don't like your attitude; I don't like your tattoos, and I don't like your face. Now get back to work."

"Fair enough, I came here as a worker to apologise, but I am now here as the union rep. Punish me if you thought I stepped out of line, but Calvin has done nothing wrong. Can you let him have his holiday back, that he booked weeks in advance? I'm pretty sure it's against the Geneva convention for group punishment."

Acting a smart cunt was not the way to his heart.

"He will not be getting his holiday now under any circumstances, and if either of you don't appear tomorrow then it will be down as gross misconduct. I know your flippant request was an innuendo for you not being in tomorrow. Now, get out of the office." He practically screamed this, and he looked like he was barely containing himself from throttling me. I have always rebelled against any authority in my life and now was not going to be any different. Fuck it, I thought.

"Oh well, you will just have to shut another line down then.

I'm away home with stress and to look up the meaning of innuendo, if you know what I mean." Whilst wagging my eyebrows.

I left him there choking on his own words, unable to form a reply due to his rage. I went down and apologised to Calvin and told the boys I was away home. I had taken five grams of ching into work that night and had sold three. It was two in the morning on a Saturday night, so I made a plan. I walked out of SPL for the final time that night, and instead of going home, I went to a friend's party I knew to be in full swing. Less than an hour later I smoked crack for the first time.

Interlude – Thirteenth Step

My family have been encouraging me to go to AA or Narcotics Anonymous, but I don't think I could stomach the "accepting god" shite they start you out on. Twelve steps? I think I'm just going to do the thirteenth step. Full-blown relapse, 'cos I can't live like this. I can't find pleasure in anything. There are thirteen steps down my house stairs from my bedroom to the bathroom, where I died. I'm hovering over the edge here.

I don't like writing down the voices I hear when I am lucid, because it makes them real. Words are thoughts given birth, and I don't want them brought into this world. I have been off drugs for months, but I got a full dose of madness today. Not even madness; I have come to think it reality again. My conversation with a mist wraith went like this.

"Flick the wheel into that car."

I got a fright and paused the music coming from the car radio.

"Turn the car into oncoming traffic. The car will come to a sudden halt, but you will continue to be propelled into such a life as you have never known."

"Who are you?"

"Immaterial and irrelevant question. You won't regret what I have asked of you." Then this is the last of the sickly-sweet voice I heard.

I drove home, shaking, took four sleeping tablets and passed out. Most conversations go like this. Full auditory conversations and never in the same voice. Each one is terrifying.

It's like it's the eleventh hour all day, every day. The edge of a cliff with a knot in your stomach, feeling there is a decision you have to make, but you don't know what.

My beautiful wife – how I have scorned her, and I deserve the hell that follows. No one do I owe more to, and nothing has made her stop loving me. How? I do not deserve it. The things I have done to her and put her through eat up my insides and tear my conscience to shreds. The first trick I pulled on her is that we are soulmates, but I sold my soul long ago. I let her fall in love with a sad, lost boy and then marry a corpse. I owe her my life. That currency doesn't have much weight, but it is owed and much more. Everything I do now I do for her.

September 10

Memento mori – remember you must die. What if you remember dying?

Life imitates art. Not long ago, I watched *Fight Club*, then the next night I was on the drink. I picked a fight with a group of boys that I knew I couldn't win. The boy pulled a knife like he was pretending to rob a bank with a banana. I ran at him headfirst, my dad trying to pull me back. My dad was only guilted into walking me home in case I took drugs or shagged anyone I shouldn't. I didn't even swing a punch, just took the first right hook like a lover's kiss, bounced on the concrete-like canvas then shouted "Weeeeee" like a fucking lunatic. I then got several kicks to my ribs that I'm pretty sure were broken. Then a volley to the head. His boot just missed the temple, inaccurate, faithless cunt.

Lunatic was right, because I didn't go home to a happy home. The one time I can explain my swollen face and blood-covered clothes, I can't. Because I am lying to her about what matters the most. I still want to die.

Cocaine really is a buffer to being steaming drunk. No way would this have happened on coke. It keeps you alert, keeps you happy and you can drink more. Every time I have ended up in trouble recently, is because of drinking and not taking gear. I never did die by taking too much drink, mind you.

A monkey doesn't let go of one branch till he has hold of the next. Owwwwwww. I was confined to the couch, and of all things I managed to spill roasting hot spaghetti carbonara all over me. I'm pretty sure I had third degree burns all over my chest, but I managed to clean up the crime scene like *Dexter*. Scrubbed the carpet, flipped the couch covers but my skin was peeling off. Along with the kicking I took earlier in the night. Who cares – I now have a bag of ching.

When someone holds up a mirror to me, I'm not afraid to look or to shatter it if it doesn't suit my skewed view.

September 14

I have been caught again: another positive test. They have been testing me intermittently, but what I have been doing is buying drugs then saving them, like a squirrel hiding his nuts for winter. Showing massive amounts of restraint by keeping them on my person and not wolfing them down. Waiting till they tested me. It would show a negative, then I would go straight to the bathroom. Gambling on the gear being out of my system by the next test.

Well, it's not worked this time. I have had more doping scandals than Neil Armstrong. I think this is it for me and my wife. I have pushed her as far as you can push a person. She has bowed in the wind but now she has broken. I have broken her and I am ashamed. She has to cut me out now for my kids' sake. I am a cancer, and I can't help myself. She has been pushing me for rehab, but I have said no, no, no.

But maybe I am ready to say yes now. Who am I kidding – I'm backed into a corner and it's my only option.

My uncle emigrated to Spain recently; maybe I will go stay with him for a while. Get out of this hole. I have too many webs and connections here and I know my contacts on Telegram won't deliver internationally. Spotlight is shining on the dark web again.

A tan might help my sickly pallor. Go be a junkie in exile; better than rehab or the Craig (local sanatorium).

Try not to make any friends or contacts out there. Knowing me, I will end up like the Peru Two.

We will see. After all, I can quit any day I want, as long as it's tomorrow.

September 30, still in fucking Alness

I never felt the struggle fat cunts feel till I quit drugs. I always used to pride myself on five foot ten, eleven stone. Once I quit the drugs and moved in with my parents, my weight ballooned to thirteen. I don't know if it was the lack of cocaine or the abundance of my Gran's bacon rolls, but I turned into a fat bastard.

Three months down the line of intermittent sobriety, and when I see my mates again, first thing I get is, "You look fat now."

Well, low and behold, I have put on a few pounds. I'm thirty-five now, and it's a shame to say that I quit football in about my thirties. Two games of fives and two training sessions plus a game at the weekend really keeps you thin. When I got too old to play, the drugs took up the slack. And they really took it up. I was more committed to sniffing lines that I ever was to doing laps of the pitch. Five years later and I am training hard on the coke. Workouts morning, noon and night, religiously.

This came to an end, like all good things do, with my death. My head clears three months later, and I am two stone heavier. But don't worry, I'm going out running tomorrow. Or on a crack binge, whatever floats your boat. Why is it acceptable for a long-distance runner to stitch his void shut by eating up the miles, whereas my chemical romance is not? Both are obsessions, and society is not who I allow to be my jury on which one I am allowed to choose. Libertarian is the romantic word I give myself. Junkie is the reality.

Some new addiction will take up the slack, I hope. I don't know if I can relapse again. My nine lives are spent with my wife. She is the real victim in all of this, and I will never forgive myself. She has been through it all with me, a guardian angel on my shoulder. Every time I have collapsed from drugs, she has been there to nurse me to health. Until my final overdose, she never knew the cause of them and even when she did, she still stood by me. Never stopping me seeing my kids, even though finding your husband on the floor covered in blood with a syringe in his arm would be grounds for divorce for anyone else.

Before my mental health deteriorated, I was a cunt leaving her to fend for herself with a new-born. Then when everything went to hell, I was never there for her during her second pregnancy when she needed me the most. I was unbelievably high when my second son was born, even getting a dealer to meet me in the hospital carpark because the birth took too long. Of all the things I hate myself for, this is the worst. Not being able to support her the way she supported me is at the top of my long list of sins, and it is the hardest one to make amends for.

We bicker and fight and scream at each other when I am home, over petty things, but I know she resents me for what I have done and is only putting up with me for our kids. There is no doubt she has post-traumatic stress from my death. Every bump in the night she bolts awake and looks for me, thinking I am dying again. Every time I am five minutes late from returning home, my pockets are emptied, and I am frisked for drugs.

I am subjected to constant drug tests and accusations. These grate on me unbelievably, but I have to fight my innate urge to rebel, as I don't have a leg to stand on any more. And they are right. If I were not under such close scrutiny, I would still be at it. Am I really in recovery, or is it just that all means have been taken away from me to take coke peacefully? This is an artificial cure to my addiction, and it cannot last forever. There are two wolves inside of me and both want coke. I don't feel recovered. I am consenting to the demeaning restriction on my life, but I still want to die. The voice in my head still whispers, jump!

Unholy Trinity

All I could see was mist, but my pain was gone. I was lying on my stomach with the fog swirling over my body, not washing away my sins but filling me up with what felt like pure adrenalin. I felt invigorated and full of life. Below me, my body was lying on the floor in a near perfect image of me above. My wife and the paramedics were gone, and the pool of blood had spread around my whole body now. My skin looked the colour of a cold December sky. I stood up in the fog quickly, surprised at the vigour in my legs and muscles. I could see out of both eyes now, and when I felt my face, all my injuries had disappeared. More than that, my nose felt straighter than it had in years. Knots in my stomach and mind I had been suffering with for decades felt like they had unravelled.

I recognised the feeling in me: it was the old Friday feeling. The excitement of a weekend that had limitless possibilities. Drink and drugs with your friends that could lead anywhere you wished. The pursuit of a new girl and the chance of sex. The wolf giving chase to the white flash of tail. Money in your pocket and a gram in your wallet. My body was nearly vibrating with this urgent feeling.

It was wrong. It was this state of mind that led me to my overdose below. I knew that, but knowledge could barely register in my mind over the powerful Friday feeling I had long sought solace in.

My surroundings had reverted to my first arrival, with the

exception of mist instead of water. Ankle-deep fog and a blanket of stars was all I could see. There was no sign of Rand or Bill, and the starlight did not seem natural any more. It seeped out with a sickly red hue. As soon as I noticed it, I could feel the starlight on my skin. It slowed the vibration I felt inside and stripped away the joy I had been feeling. The trepidation rose inside me, and I spun in circles, looking for anything to help. I could not bring myself to look down again. I knew my body had died and I had lost. Below was my corpse, and I was trapped above it, a tormented ghost.

Thoughts of being trapped here alone for eternity flashed through my head. How long till I went completely insane? I had no direction to run, nothing on the surrounding horizon and nothing to bash my head against. With no other option, I screamed my throat hoarse. Nothing answered me, and the violent starlight muffled my terror screams as soon as they left my lips. I began to beg and plead, calling Rand and Bill for another chance. I sank to my knees and prayed, to whom or what I didn't care. Thoughts of every drug I had taken, every stupid decision I had ever made, every time I dove into my stupid party lifestyle, every time I lived up to the expectations of Party Marty, every time I chose drink and drugs over my family streamed through my head, and I cursed them all.

I realised I was crying. For the first time in seventeen years, I was crying. I thought back to the last time, and the tears came harder. With the little strength I had left, I whispered a final prayer.

It was answered but not by what I expected. A nightmare rose from the fog in front of me. An incorporeal shifting body of a man, made entirely from the mists and flowing in strange patterns. Its head was the horror. Or heads, as there were three, not made of mist but attached to the body. A three-headed wolf grinned at me, each jaw dripping with malice. Six eyes, the colour of the violet stars, stared me down, and I shrank back. Cowering behind nothing, the feeling of death gripped me again. Jet-black fur bristled on each head. Three jaws lined with too-white teeth. Three gaping maws sucking in the mist and exhaling fear.

"Hello, again," Rand said, his voice coming from all three wolf heads. "You are not very good at this, are you? And here we are, exiled from your body and denied a return to the whole. You will stagnate here forever."

"Where is Bill? Please, where is Bill? I need one more chance."

"Bill can't help you now, but I can. See, I never really wanted you to lose. Say my name, and I will give you one last chance." Rand's voice almost seemed genuine, but he still radiated death.

"Rand."

"Ehhh-errrr. Try again. Come now, I heard your last prayer, whispered to no one. Say my name."

He was right, I knew. I just couldn't bring myself to face it. On my hands and knees in the fog, I looked down at my dead body. Frozen in time forever. I raised my head and whispered, "Me, you are me. Martin."

"Ding ding ding, we have a winner. I am you, and you are me; congratulations to both of us." His, or my, voice was back to its jovial past.

"I am the demon inside of you. You have known it from the moment you laid eyes on me; you just refused to admit it. I am the addictions you have collected proudly; I am the surge of serotonin you get from a good line; I am the gnawing feeling telling you that enough is not enough; I am the urge to self-destruct; I am the hollowness you feel with life. I am the voice that whispers, jump. In short, I am the damaged you in all its glory. Your first step has been taken in admitting what we are. You still have not figured out where we came from. But you prayed for one last chance, and if you don't ask, you don't get, shy boys don't get sweeties. So, take it away, get us out of here so we can celebrate," he said, winking at me.

I could almost sense an undertone of pleading in his voice. He was the worst part of me, and I knew not to trust even the best part. Bill had not appeared when it was him I had sent my prayers to, and I now knew why. I closed my eyes and the mist claimed me.

DUALITY

I am a teenager again but it ain't a good night. It is one of those nights where you are wrestling with the covers. A day of drinking and taking speed is the culprit. Now that I have crashed, I am exhausted, but sleep is elusive. The speed is still in my system, so I toss and turn in bed, thrashing the covers about. Lie and stare at the ceiling, feeling my hangover build. What makes it worse, my girlfriend is snoring contentedly next to me. I shake her awake just for someone to talk to.

"Fuck sake, Mart, what is it?"

"I can't sleep. Can I get my hole?"

"Fuck off. You wouldn't even be able to get it up anyway; you were hoovering up any speed in sight at the party."

"Listen, no matter how many drugs I take, I can still split you like kindling."

"Fuck off and let me sleep." I could tell that tone, so I let her be and went back to starting at my spot on the ceiling.

A staring contest with agitation and win or lose, the prize is restlessness and anxiety. My phone goes and I sit bolt upright in bed, grab it and get blinded by the screen light. There is only one reason my phone would go at this time of night. My grand'a.

My grand'a is a small man but large in personality. A born-and-bred Glaswegian. A Weegie who grew up on Hill Head, a Blue Nose and a Mason (Celtic conspiracy theorists love when these two go hand in hand). He is short, with a weathered face and thick black hair gone grey that he has held well into old age.

My earliest memory of him is going for long walks in the woods around my parents' house, him watching me build dens and swings (training for the death slides and Ewok village me and Andy would construct in our teens) and spinning off-the-cuff stories about dragons and monsters with us as the heroes who save the day. I idolised him and latched onto him like a shadow. He was kind and witty and spoke to me as a friend and never as an authority figure.

He would bleather to me for hours, talking about football, cunts he hates, people he likes, just getting the craic to someone fifty years his junior. All this spoken in his, exotic-sounding to me, Glaswegian accent he held on to, despite living in the Highlands for two decades. Rumours, political opinion and strange, cryptic statements flowing out of him were the norm. No wonder he got kicked out of the Masons for spilling secrets.

Things like after I told him a story about me falling out with someone at school he would reply, "Have ya seen the nick of that cunt? Tell him to away an take his face for a shite." Then to have my gran tell him to shut his dish around the wains.

Or, "If that weird-looking crater's legs were straight, he would be eight foot tall."

He used to tell me his dad was killed by a giant crab, and a ten-year-old me never questioned this, always on the lookout for one of these monsters at any beach I visited. It was only years later I realised he meant cancer.

The two that stuck with me the most but still make no sense decades later…

"Aye, well, we will meet again one day for high tea. Up a hill," and, "Upon a hill there stood a coo, it musta shifted, 'cos it's no there noo." Baffling. I think he just liked to wind me up.

He had spent most of his adult life working in Dalmore

107

Distillery, and from the stories he and my gran have told me, it was just another boys' club, albeit in a different era.

Being drunk at work on their own whisky was the norm. They would all carry around white napkins and drink the plus sixty per cent black barrel proof whisky through this. By the end of the day, everyone's napkins would be black and their faces red. Hip flasks would be taken home and the cycle continued. My gran once told me the minister visited my grand'a before a service one Sunday to try and coerce him into joining his flock. My grand'a proved himself an unruly wolf and got the minister so drunk on his personal stash that the minister fell flat on his face during his own service.

I never really grasped that my grand'a was sick until I got a bit older. Our walks got shorter and then not at all. He became housebound and needed oxygen tubes running to his nose from a tank he trailed behind him. Like a leash held by the Reaper. Eventually he became confined to an armchair in his living room. From the age of thirteen and up, this is where I would see him, visiting him every day after school to watch TV with him or play boardgames.

Always attached to oxygen tubes, always in the same armchair, always with a dram in hand and a smile on his face.

He had tuberculosis and was diagnosed not long before I was born. He was in isolation for months and was not allowed to see his first grandchild without a plastic screen wall between us. I was inoculated early and all my family given boosters. When it was determined that he was not contagious, he was released from the perspex prison and allowed to hold me, and to be honest, he has never let go.

His case was complicated and at the time untreatable. The disease would eat a chunk of his lung then go into hiding for months or even years. Sometimes it only took a small bite and other times it was ravenous. It withered him away, melting flesh off his bones and chewing his insides.

He had a demon inside of him that ate the very breath from his lungs, but he took it all in his stride with a smile on his face. He was dancing with the Reaper, never knowing when the music would end. Not giving a fuck and dancing to his own tune. The bravest man I ever knew.

It was the asbestos in the distillery that caused it, although it could never be proven.

It was my mum on the phone.

"What's wrong?" But I knew the answer.

"He's fallen again; come quick."

As I got older and my grand'a's condition worsened, I slowly became his carer, as he didn't have the energy to walk any more. He still lived in his own house with my gran, but she didn't have the strength to carry him, even though he was as light as a feather. When he needed help to move from the bed to his armchair in the living room or from the armchair to his wheelchair or even to the toilet, I was there to carry him. Every day I would get up, go up and help my grand'a get dressed and move him to his armchair, go to school, piss off some teachers, go back to my grand'a's for dinner and help him get ready for bed, then either go home and piss off my parents or piss off my girlfriend.

I was happy, mischievous and a wind-up merchant. My grand'a actively encouraged this, loving the craic when I would tell him about how I got detention that day by sawing the legs of a teacher's chair slightly in half, so when he leaned back it would snap. I was a class clown and revelled in it, only getting let off with shit because my grades were good. By the time I was in the sixth year, all the kids in my year that had stayed on were prefects, and I was still on fucking toilet cards. My reputation had started to precede me, and once on a bus going to a footy game for school, we were playing travel scrabble.

"Think I've lost an e, sir."

"No like ya," our PE teacher quipped. Haha; I could do nothing but laugh.

My school was filled with wee cunts like me. It was small but it was wild. I mind one day a boy brought a sheep into our common area from a nearby field, and they were all practising wrestling moves on it. Poor sheep was getting a pile driver off a class table.

My grand'a loved stories like these. He thrived on them, and I think it kept him going far longer than TB had planned for him. I don't think he could go either until he converted me into a full Blue Nose. He was in a tug-of-war competition with my dad, who is originally from Perth and a St Johnstone fan. My dad would take me to an away game in Monaco, and my grand'a would arrange for me to go to a Rangers training camp in Largs. I hate to admit it though, Dad, but the Gers won.

My dad will always be content with the fact that I forever will be an SNP supporter and pro-independence. Scotland should be free; no two ways about it in my eyes. There is a reason the unicorn is in chains on my passport, and it is because we are slaves still. How can any politics be valid in Scotland if no matter how we vote, the sheer number of English voters can just overrule us and do as they wish? Hence, two decades of Tory rule, Brexit and this Orwellian state we are living in.

But I digress. If my patriotism is strong, then my dad's is through the roof. Just like how *Trainspotting* ripped the piss outa Rangers fans for having their PIN numbers as 1690 for the Battle of the Boyne, his PIN for everything is 1314 for the Declaration of Arbroath. The whole Declaration is engraved on a stone outside our family house. He has a picture of Nicola Sturgeon on his wall and he sleeps with a Claymore under his bed.

These were the happiest times of my life. I was young, had all my family around me, excellent grades, average at football, a girlfriend I could get a ride from and the thrill of the chase for other girls at the weekend. Drink and drugs were still new. I had an affinity with current music, with Oasis and The View, and most importantly, my inner demon was still in adolescence. Then it was all ripped away.

"Marty, hurry, it's bad."

I played football a lot and could average a mile in seven minutes, but from the second I dropped that phone, I ran the mile from my parents' to my grand'a's in under five. When I arrived, my mum and Gran were both in hysterics. He had fallen out of bed and was in an awkward position, and he would scream and shout if either of them made an attempt to lift him. He was now in palliative care; bedbound other than the rare days I could coax him downstairs to his armchair.

I scooped him up, a bag of bones, and he shouted at me in anger, maybe the first time he had ever raised his voice to me in nineteen years.

"Just let me die in peace."

Then a whisper, "Just let me die in peace."

I felt a pull inside me, something trying to rip me back to purgatory. My nineteen-year-old self-ignored it, instinct knowing there was something more to come.

He died the next night in his own bed as he had wished, surrounded by our family and a nurse, who quietly nodded as she took the non-existent pulse. It was 4/4/4, and I have hated the number ever since. Never going out on that day, never having it showing on the volume of a TV, never betting on that horse, and in the midst of my gambling addiction never betting on four on the roulette. The solitary number with no chips on it compared with the tower of chips heaped on every other number on the roulette table.

I was numb. I knew this day was coming but never thought it would. We all hugged, my poor sister bawling her eyes out, my mum and Gran inconsolable. I never even shed a tear. My world had been ripped apart, and I was angry, not sad. Furious at any God that would let a kind, caring and brave man die in such prolonged agony. Everyone remained in the room with the corpse. I needed to be alone. That thing was no longer my grand'a, and I needed to get away.

I went downstairs and sat in his armchair with my head in my hands. The only thoughts in my head were of how steaming I could get and how many drugs I would take to kill the pain inside. I sat there in silence and then it hit me. It started in the base of my spine and rose up my body. Filling me fit to burst. The only experience I could relate to it at the time was coming up on ecstasy. It was akin to the goosebumps you feel when your body resonates with a piece of music, or the welling of emotion you see when your child comes into this world. Only much stronger, a hard-line to the Divine instead of information picked up on the radio waves.

I knew it was my grand'a's soul, waiting to comfort me, sitting in his old armchair, knowing I would come and sit in the exact same spot. The feeling left as quickly as it had come. No words were passed. I saw no spooky apparition and no supposed light at the end of the tunnel with him waving from the beyond. But I was left with facts. Undeniable truths embedded inside me that there is more to this life. I had felt my grand'a in the afterlife and was given the merest snippet of the joy he was feeling.

It's hard to claim something like this with no irrefutable evidence, but my grand'a waited to fill me with answers. He was at peace. There is never anything to fear, as death is but a door. One we all must open to be greeted by the greater part of ourselves. We are all slivers of infinity. The gift I was given faded as fast as it came, the affinity I felt to everything narrowed to my own pain and what I had lost. Not just my grand'a but what he let me feel, what he was a part of. A greater whole, shattered into billions of sentient lives. Each part experiencing its life subjectively before returning home.

I stood up out of his chair and smiled. I was happy for him and knew we would meet again for high tea up a hill. Then I was torn away from this memory back to the personal hell I had created and the fresh knowledge of the gift I had squandered.

Interlude – The Darkness Consumes You

October 19

Is it better to be in hell with the hope of salvation, the anticipation of a high to come? Or high with the constant fear of the inevitable fall? There is no middle ground, and to live in mediocrity is a sin.

I have gone through withdrawals for a few things now: crack, coke, nicotine, valium, (Queens of the Stone Age here), dihydrocodeine, xanax and so many antidepressants and mood stabilisers I have lost count. But let me tell you, pregabalin is the worst. If you want to abuse it smart, then you can take four or five tablets at once and feel euphoric for a day. Give it three days' rest, as your tolerance drops really quickly, then start the cycle again. I was taking eight just to get out of bed in the morning. Another eight on my first tea break at work then another eight on my second, six hours later. I did this for over a year. A year of being insulated from the outside world. You stop getting the euphoric feeling after a few days of constant use. You are left with the feeling of confidence it gives you. Dulled nerves – I would burn myself at work and hardly feel it. But overall contentment. Happy with your lot in life, no matter how shitty it is. When all that is taken away, it's like a living hell.

The withdrawal starts the minute you take your last pill, as you know it's your last, and your anxiety flares up along with a guttural fear. Like the sun is dying, and all you can do is watch.

114

The physical withdrawal starts a few days after. Nausea, sweats, shakes. Tremors so bad you are unable to type on your phone. Shitting and spewing out everything you have eaten in the last decade. And your nerves. Everything is too loud, too bright, too rough, too hard, too life. I remember going for a shower and crying due to the pain of the water hitting my back. You have been skinned alive and left open to the elements. Naked in the dark.

Goblins have become quite common now. Well, common within the underworld of society. I was a prodigy in this respect. Years ago, I was ordering sleeping tablets off a site online and noticed them for sale. Like an impulse buyer, I would add random drugs to my shopping cart to see if they had a good high. These were one of them. What a good pick. They blew my head off the first time I took them and I was getting them for pennies on the dollar. When I was prescribed something that I was already addicted to, all I could do was laugh.

A rolling stone gathers no moss; static breeds rot. A moving mind is always fed; at mind at rest devours itself.

It's hard being a junkie man. Especially on a budget. Every waking hour is spent high or hunting the means to get high. I was fortunate to fall in the middle of the slider where my appetite outstripped my means. And that included the paper tower of drug dealers and tricks I set up, plus a considerable debt. Unlimited money, and I would be dead. I nearly was, anyway. The other end of the scale and it is just fortunate for everyone. I would have made a terrible rent boy.

Is your love for something or someone diminished because you risk losing it? Does being born with no survival instincts and no fear of consequences make your love worthless? I don't think there is a threshold of love I could cross that would make me forego the risks of its loss. Even trivial risk is taken without a second thought. Maybe I am just broken.

Pleiades

I opened my eyes and Bill was standing in front of me. I was still standing in water, but the stars had disappeared, to be replaced by a brilliant vanilla sky.

"So, now you know," Bill said quietly.

I used to stargaze as a kid. The light pollution by my parents' house is non-existent. A coach house built in 1703, it is surrounded by woodland. My bedroom had a skylight, and at night I had the whole universe in the palm of my hand. I would lie on my bed for hours, imagining myself living on distant planets and exploring new worlds. I could name all the constellations in my hemisphere and had star maps on my bedroom walls. I was a curious wee fucker and was obsessed with how the pyramids were built and how they aligned with Orion's Belt, how the Egyptians worshipped the sun god Ra and the amazing similarities Ra has with Christ.

My obsession with stars grew as I religiously watched *The X Files*. I was convinced of extra-terrestrial life and that our planet was seeded from the stars, more specifically, the Pleiades, or the seven sisters as they are also known. It is a star cluster close to Earth with seven of the brightest stars clearly visible in the night sky. I don't know why they held such significance to me, but if I am out at night, they always draw my eye and I stare longingly at them, unconsciously wishing them to pull me away to a happier life.

I gazed into the stars that formed Bill's face. With the

Pleiades slowly sailing across his features, the realisation grew in me. The stars faded and his features took form. It was my grand'a, not the rotten vessel the disease had left him but his true form. A healthy young man with a twinkle in his eye. I threw my arms around him and burst into tears. Emotions I had been bottling up for fifteen years flowed out of me like poison. My grand'a was my shining knight and seeing him again had lanced my wound.

My grand'a hugged me back, gripping me tight. "Hey, Tommy boy, how you keeping?" he said. Tommy boy was the hero of all the stories he told me when I was young.

"This memory can destroy, and you have let it. I am so sorry for what I said. You have let the wrong part of this memory embed itself so deep in your head that you forgot it was there. It has been the deciding factor every time you are faced with a crisis. Fuck it, you think, let me die in peace.

"You think it is freedom not fearing death, but it has shackled you from ever truly living, making real connections, fully loving something without fear of losing it. You have sought out people and literature that reinforce this shard of a memory. Only when we have lost everything are we free to do anything, you have read. You have kept life at a distance and thought yourself brave. But you are a coward for not remembering the true part of this memory. The love and exaltation you felt, the undeniable truth you were allowed a glimpse of. Souls are eternal and death is a doorway does not mean you squander the life you have. It should be the axis which you revolve a happy life around, not one casually flaunting death because you think you have a safety net."

I had never been scolded by my grand'a before. I didn't know what to feel. So many conflicting emotions warring inside of me. The happiness at seeing him again, the joy at the sliver of eternity he had shown me, the shock at the anger in his voice showing me the mistake I had made and the gut-wrenching shame knowing that he had seen my life in its entirety. All my sins laid bare, skeletons pulled out of the closet, bodies dug up from under the patio.

"It is okay, my boy, it is all okay," he said, as if reading my thoughts.

"It's time for a change. Make the choice: go back to your gorgeous wife, who has stood by you through so much. Do you know, I knew her Granny? We would go to the lung clinic together, her for her cancer and me for my TB. We sat together, fighting death, never knowing we would share three great grandkids. You can find evil or beauty in that. It's strange the way the world works. Go back to my great grandkids I have watched grow. Make the right choice and make it stick. Let go of your hate towards the world and just let yourself be happy. Goodbye. I love you, Tommy boy."

And with that, he left me again. No slowly fading away or a dramatic flair into a shower of stars.

The stars around me began to pulse, the beat quickening until they were a lone blinding light and me in a tunnel of darkness. The light at the end of the tunnel went out, for this was no tunnel. It was syringe full of drugs. The plunger went down and I was pushed back, through the needle. My thoughts were stretched thin. Back into my own veins and bringing myself to life.

I awoke in blood.

Take Me to the Top (And Throw Me Off)

My wife found me dead on my bathroom floor. Needle still sticking out of my arm, a bag of coke and a spoon stuffed in my pocket. The paramedics arrived and removed the needle from my arm, and the police arrived and stole my drugs. When I opened my eyes, my wife screamed. The paramedic rushed me to hospital, away from the carnage I had caused. My dad rode in the ambulance with me I think. My memory on this is a bit hazy, you see. I had got greedy, ran too fast to try and catch that carrot the monkey was dangling.

I had shot up so much coke it caused me to go into a violent seizure. A full tonic-clonicseizure with the normal accompanying blood-curdling scream. I landed on the hard granite floor. My convulsions repeatedly smacked my head into the floor, shattering my eye socket and breaking my nose. Then I died. I came back again almost instantly with the sense thoroughly knocked into me. Life really does flash before your eyes, I was given a choice and I made it. But will it stick?

I remember everything that happened to me in purgatory, my memory not jogged but sprinted at truths I needed reminding of. Lying in the hospital listening to the beeps of the machines I was wired to, I thought about everything that had happened. Every memory I had been reminded of, every misdeed I had gotten away with, every time I had fucked over my family on my crusade of martyrdom.

I thought of my sore face, the throbbing from the collapsed vein where the needle had been stuck in through a seizure. I thought of the ache in my entire body from dying. I thought of how I had to change, how I had to be better, how I had to do this for my wife and sons and for my grand'a, who I knew was watching me. But there was one thing I thought of the most.

The bag of drugs the fucking pigs who arrived with the ambulance had stolen from me.

C'est la vie – such is life. An addict in a nutshell. The whole world on offer, limitless possibilities for happiness, but weigh it against a quick fix and the latter will win every time. This is going to be fucking hard.

I had found my truths the hard way, but that was easy compared to what was to follow. I still don't think I had found the answers I needed. This wasn't over, or maybe I just didn't want it to be.

A Perfect Storm

November

The butterfly's wings that cause a hurricane. That's what the little choices are on the road to being a junkie. Just a few lines with a pint. A wee baggy to take to nightshift. A big line to do the housework. Bump this bill to buy a half q. Borrow off my parents to pay my tic. Shoot up to shut out the noise in my skull. A slippery slope when phrased like that: you only think of how easy it is to slide down. Not the near impossible feat of climbing back up.

Party Marty is dead. He died when my head hit the cold mortuary slab in my downstairs bathroom. When the lights went out, I went into a cocoon. My slow recovery from addiction, relapses included, has occurred in a self-induced coma from the world. Four months on, I'm still not prepared to push through the membrane, reveal who I have become. I am scared I have just evolved into something worse. Less jovial and more sinister. No longer the devil's jester but the devil himself, interested in no one's death but his own.

I have started a health kick. Off running in the woods to give my body good endorphins. That's the cover anyway. Not a cover but a curtain, and behind the curtain is a junkie wizard who just wanted time alone so he could shoot up. Alness really is in a beautiful place. The Scottish Highlands have a feel like no other. Having lived in the Canadian Rockies, I can attest to this.

Maybe it is just because it is home. There is a documented

proof of this. Generations grow up and move to the cities for their youth but always return to the Highlands to lay roots and grow a family of their own. I can see Fyrish in the distance. A rolling hill with a huge arched gateway built on top as a monument. I always joked that it was the gateway to hell and had secret thoughts of a drug-fuelled suicide ending hanging on that gate.

I pull my eyes away from that thought and back to the trees surrounding me. I loved the woods as a kid. Untold hours climbing trees and making swings filled my youth. I always felt at home surrounded by trees. At peace. I feel like an intruder now, sitting behind a tree with a bottle cap full of cocaine. Like an explorer, my needle always finds true north. Drawn to the iron in my blood, like a magnet. The rush of drugs and I am an intruder no longer but part of nature itself. This feeling is so natural. Why does the whole world insist it is wrong? Am I a coward to bow to their demands and stay clean, or a coward to hide from the world behind my veil of drugs?

Fuck it; for the moment I'm part of these woods and no one can see the forest for the trees.

I became a twin sometime in my early teens. The first generation to be given an electrical surrogate, marriage of metal and flesh separated by clothing, skin and air, but a perfect merging of consciousness. Not just of mine to my phone, but mine to the global surge all jacked in. If you do not keep your feet on this path then you are swept away, forever lost to the growing hive mind.

What started as a cheap but indestructible Nokia 3310 slowly grew with me but evolved at a much faster rate into my newest edition iPhone. In all the years since I was given my twin, we have never been apart for a night. Never separated for more than a few hours and even these short periods by accident. A few hours result in separation anxiety.

What this has resulted in is every major milestone in my life being documented by pictures. Every occasion I deemed exciting enough I have photos for. I have been diligent in transferring pics from phone to phone, from phone to laptop and eventually from laptop to cloud. An unbroken stream of photos and videos for over twenty years of my life. A digital flow of consciousness. If viewed fast enough, you can see my threads unravelling. My sanity coming apart at the seams.

In our pockets we have the means to access all of mankind's collected knowledge. It blows my mind. It should have liberated us as a species, but it has enslaved us. Me more than most, as just a few clicks on my phone and I can have any drugs on the planet delivered to my door. How does one stay strong with that temptation to hand? I was a veteran of the rise of bitcoin then the demise of Silk Road.

What it has evolved into now is so much easier. PCs are not needed; you don't need to hide your digital footprint with a VPN; you don't have to connect via The Onion Router. You don't even have to pay with bitcoin any more. What was once a convoluted process that only a small percentage of drug users could navigate has now been compressed into an app on your phone. Open the app and once you have been added to the right groups, there is a list of verified vendors offering every drug and service imaginable. I could order an ounce of high-purity coke in the morning, have it arrived in a vacuum-sealed pack by the Royal Mail the next day, turn the ounce with a little cutting agent and short-changing bags into thirty-five grams and make a two thousand two hundred profit.

I know people who have capitalised very well on this, but to me it was buy a half ounce, get it into bags then go one for you, two to me with every customer I met. I never did more than break-even: monetary gain was never the motivator for me. Staying constantly high was why I loved this new advent of technology. It was like a treadmill I couldn't get off. A monkey riding the back of a donkey by using a carrot on a stick the donkey would never reach. I was both donkey and carrot, and the monkey was on my back.

I got so deeply involved, and with the amount of pregabalin and Ching I was buying, I ended up on first name terms with a few of the major wholesalers, even ending up in a separate Telegram group for high stakes poker. I have always loved poker and I won more than I lost in these games, but the profits went straight back to the other players with me buying more drugs, so is that really winning? Is it fuck?

Addiction had now permeated every aspect of my life. Everything I once enjoyed was now overshadowed by narcotics. How can I cut the bad things out my life if every single thing I do revolves around drugs? Do I cut my whole life out? I cannot be a junkie if I am dead. Anyway, I am starting to feel the world again: time for more goblins.

The naivety of it all. I can see now there was a monster growing inside of me and all I did was feed it, never once stopping to take stock of my feelings or those around me. Trusting my instincts when I should have been listening to what my mind what trying to tell me. It's a dark world out there, and when you manage to shine a light on it, illuminating something of value, the light takes away your night vision and leaves you in deeper shadows. Here they be monsters. This rockstar life on a pauper's budget you have orchestrated in your mind is a sham. King for a day, skint for the rest of the week. It's pitiful.

November 20
My mind is trying to kill me

There are times when reality is nothing but pain and in order to deal with the pain, we must leave reality behind. Then there is death. I have fear from ignorance. My unfounded fear of something I could not name let alone understand means I can never kill my fear. Terrified Infiniti. As above so below

A cunt knows a cunt. And I am.

White straight male privilege and don't I know it. I'm sure if I had to walk 5 miles for dysentery infested water to feed my kids that would die before they are old, I would feel real sorrow. But I don't, I'm just a depressed junkie stuck in a vicious cycle on my homeland paradise. A battery to the capitalist regime, unable to break free unless blessed with divine talent. Alas my talent was cursed by the devil. Self-destruction is the most addictive drug I've known. I should know, I've tried them all. Even my own self-pity grates on me. I am going to burn this page and use it to light my crack. And I've just noticed how grey my hair has turned during this ordeal, burned in times fire.

I should have died on my bathroom floor. Everyday since I woke up, I have been in pain or caused my family anguish. It's a cruel joke being played on me this shot at redemption. Some twisted god is laughing at my struggle. A rabbit thrashing in a snare only making it tighter. My veins are tighter. Constricted from shooting up my life. Trading years with my family for minutes of relief. My psychiatrist says I've had a psychotic break. If I told her the half of it I would be in a padded room. I've been buying coke, getting needles from the fucking chemist in boots, surrounded by all the happy Christmas shoppers. An oil spill floating on a happy sea. Then I park my car in an underground parking lot and shoot up in the dark. I can do it in a flash now, blink and you will miss it. I am on the fringe of society, a separate species on the edge of the word waiting to fall off. Turtles all the way down

I got a bag off my dealer the other day and couldn't wait to get it in a vein. I just drove round the corner and parked next to a school. I rushed it and did far too much. I just got the needle out and sheathed before the world spun. My vision was going black and I had a piercing moment of clarity that this was it and I was dying. I felt utterly calm, at peace. Then the fucking world slowed down again and the fear returned. Oh, well, on with the show.

Coke ain't even doing it for me any more. I want smack before I join the great beyond. Mellow yellow to golden brown. Float down the river to the rapids then falls. We all float down here.

Fuck me I am a weak-willed cunt. Or no will. When there is no will there is no way. Why don't I want anything? Why am I empty? I was strung out on goblins last week cos the fucking postie had about three bank holidays in a row off. four days I went with no pregabalin. That's after taking ten a day for six months. It was a living hell. The mental torment is indescribable. A constant terrified undercurrent to your waking mind. No respite from this fear. I never thought fear could get that bad. I don't think I'm scared of anything. Other than spiders the spawn of Satan but this is a fear without a source. A nightmare without a face, nothing you can pin down to where the terror stems from.

Then the physical withdrawals kick in after three days. Shivers, shakes, shooting pains and the shits. I sat at the window for three days waiting for the Fucking post man. I vowed never to get like that again. Drugs are a part of me now. Intertwined with my personality and body. I don't know who I am without them and I'm too old and run down to start from scratch. All I have are these late-night ramblings on coke binges to keep the voices at bay and me in a duality. Already dead but still living for my family.

Once again, what a whiney cunt I am.

I've taken to staring at myself in the mirror when spaced out. Not in vanity, in disgust. Staring at my flaws, hating myself. I don't even think I am real any more. Is anything real. How can we even define what's real. Each mind builds their own universe for it to live in. If I asked you to describe the colour blue, you couldn't. You would have to point to it. We can agree that we both call that blue but we might not perceive the blue the same. Yes, explain the length of the light waves and how it hits the cones in your retinas if you must but how do we know the same information registers the same to us in the world our mind has created. This can be applied to anything I think. Maybe I am losing my mind. Fuck it, there is no Fucking way any of this is real. This is a simulation and I'm the main character so I'm just going to do whatever the fuck I please.

Smoking outside at night staring at the stars. I love how little light pollution there is in our highland paradise. God we are insignificant. Specks on the wind in a pale blue dot. My pain is meaningless in a universe that goes outward forever and inward as such. This knowledge doesn't lessen the pain for me just underlines how pointless my struggling is. Win or lose my battle with my demons and the result won't even register. A drop in the ocean so why fight? My sons, by god I love them. I'm scared to stay and poison them with my presence, and I'm scared to leave them.

Recovery is painful. Days stretch out far longer when you are sober. I wake up in a haze, drowsy to the point of zombification. My psychiatrist has me on a cocktail of drugs to level out my manic depression, to subdue my borderline personality disorder and to quell the auditory voices that want me to follow them down the rabbit hole. I rattle when I walk, like a tube of Smarties with all the pills inside me. The pills don't work, and my protests fall on deaf ears. Withdrawal is now underlined in all my medical notes.

I stagger to a bookcase and pull out a specific volume. Behind are my goblins, and I take ten. Three grams worth, and I am up to doing this three times a day, the worst it has ever been. Friends and family tell me they can see the change in me, that my extra weight looks good on me and that I am acting like my old self again. It's different this time, as I feel guilt for duping them. Putting on another show, masquerading as an addict in recovery when all I have done is increased one addiction to kill the other.

I still hear voices and can see the mist if I relax my vision, and I have been off cocaine for over a month now. My madness, my psychosis is not brought on by excessive cocaine use, and I don't know how that makes me feel. Happy that I wasn't such a fuck up that I took so many drugs I created a fantasy world for myself and went to live there. Or terrified that this will be a lifelong battle to stop me convening with the malevolent demons holding court in my head.

Even knowing what I know now, what has been forced down my throat, I am scared it is not enough. The lessons that were beaten into me won't stick. That instant of togetherness I felt has been diluted through the years, and my time in purgatory now feels like a bad dream. I don't know how to reconnect with what I felt, what will surely save me. Is it God? I don't think it is. What we label as God is what we are all part of. Each and every living thing a sliver of infinity.

I could never turn to the church, as I hate it with a passion. Not just because of my hatred of authority but because it is a manmade construct. Something that was once pure has been corrupted by man. Embedded with human traits, flaws and prejudice. The bible, the Koran, the Torah: I have read them all and come away feeling more jaded than when I began. Hinduism and Buddhism seemed to align more with my faith, but ultimately, they could help me no more than reading the works of William Burroughs.

I need to find the plug (not a dealer, haha) that can fill the void. A connection, even if tenuous, to the transcendent feeling I felt that night sitting in my grand'a's chair. If I stop searching, I know how it will end. I will turn to the only deity I have ever known, and his sermons involve the crux of my arm and a needle crucifix.

November 27
Tree surfing – verb
On a particularly windy day that coincides with the deep abyss of your bipolar sonograph, you pick a tree and climb until you can climb no more. Your head must breach the canopy regardless of how flimsy the branches are below your feet. Relax and sway with the forest. Watch the wind make an undulating

mass of the leaves around you. Open yourself to the world, and if what you show it causes the world to snap the trunk below you, then so be it. Fall to the embrace of the forest floor, free of fear.

I have had my tree picked out for years. I have fallen out of it drunk once, but I have never been thrown down while standing with my head and shoulders above the canopy, arms open wide.

I met one of my friends today, and she was gushing over how much healthier I looked. Fuller cheeks, a beard (to hide the developing extra chin), clothes not hanging off me like vultures on a tree. Haunted eyes, but that will never change. She is a stunning girl who works with my sister. Now a lesbian, she has been in a long-term relationship with another lesbian friend of mine. I have no prejudices at all: race, creed, colour, sexuality, it is all the same to me. Do what makes you happy as long as it is not at the detriment to others.

If everyone is equal in my eyes, then everyone can be made fun of, and Alness had a lesbian problem at one point. I think there were more lesbians in Alness than there were men, haha. We had no chance. My friend was the culprit: she was seducing women left, right and centre. We would be out in the pub and she would spot a good-looking lassie and tell me, "Call me Tina, 'cos I'm gonna Turner."

It was a pandemic. I would joke that this was the Lost Boys, she was the head vampire, and to turn back all the others she had bitten, I would need to stake her. She was far more elusive than Dracula though.

Anyway, looking and feeling healthier is not enough. I have no gym for my mind. The mask is put on to the world again.

Life is precious to me, but I longed to re-join the whole. The all-encompassing energy that we are part of but not part of at the

130

same time. Separated at birth and re-joined at death. I would not take my own life. That would be a sin. But pushing my addictions to the limits and overdosing would be cheating the system. It's nice to live without any fear of death. Liberating.

I'm high, and I know for a fact that life is precious and it's good to be alive. But it's even better to be alive on drugs. It's so much simpler being a junkie. All the nuances and stress of life are stripped away. No more worrying about your job, if your wife hates you, the voices and your dwindling grasp on sanity. All your thoughts are focused on one singular motive – to never sober up.

What is time? Have I done this before, and will I do it again? Does it matter, now that I have done it once and time is infinite? The past, future and present are one, so my act of overdosing has and always will be happening. Do I believe this, or is it just an excuse I tell myself to stay a junkie?

Yin and yang. Why can't I have a middle ground? On one hand, I'm a nervous, depressed, suicidal guy, who can't find joy in anything. On the other hand, there is a toxic junkie. Give me drugs and I am happy. The pain disappears. Why can't there be a hybrid? A guy who is content with life and doesn't feel the need to destroy everything and everyone around him.

December 20

Unless you have been there, you won't understand the struggle of intense paranoia you get when you are trying to secretly draw up a shot. Your whole world slows down and you forget to breathe, so much so you only notice it when you hear your heartbeat slow. Why can't I do things in moderation? Just get a hobby and not have it turn into an all-consuming obsession.

Just get slightly drunk and not have it led to shooting up coke and browsing for hookers. Just go slightly insane... Voices whispering to me became my friends. We are all one. Our life's energy is split from the whole. They want me to re-join the fold. I can feel everything. If I relax my eyes, I can see individual molecules floating in the air, feel the vibrations of everything around me. I long for death, for my vibration to slow and match the hum of the whole.

I'm sitting in the sun, with butterflies drifting lazily around me. I am staring at the wonder of the world, yet my eyes keep getting drawn to trees with good branches I can hang myself from. Why are these thoughts a constant throughout my mind? Why must I look the gorgon in the face?

I have been trying to learn the guitar, but all I've been doing is taking lines off the back of it. Pluck a few chords then spin the guitar over and do a few lines. I dunno how, but I've managed to learn Red Hot Chilli Peppers' "Other side" with this method.

How long, how loooong will I slide? Slitting my throat is all I ever had.

This one time I shot up, I caught my reflection in the mirror. I was so fucked I thought I looked rock 'n' roll, cool and decadent. I was nothing but a dirty bag of bones and a syringe full of drugs. I used to joke about this at parties when a group of us were taking lines off a mirror. "Don't make eye contact with the monster." Everyone would laugh, but I am not laughing now. I have seen the devil in my eyes, and he winked at me.

And this one time, at band camp, I shoved a flute in my pussy.

January 7
To call Dave boisterous would be an understatement. Loud,

132

funny and loves attention. When he gets drunk and in full swing it's the Dave Murray show. Dreams romance and excess down his ribs, he loves the view as much as me and I love him like a brother.

My other brother and third Usher at my wedding, Kenneth aka the foetus. A one of a kind, hilarious and loud. He has a weathered face; his hard paper round in Chernobyl. Once on holiday back from Ibiza he had to check the bags under his eyes in for the flight home. When him a Dave are on the drink together you need to fight to get a word in edge ways and your ears will be bleeding after five minutes in their company. Through all my troubles they have been there for me and I can never repay them. I have surrounded myself with loud funny charismatic characters and I couldn't ask for better friends.

There are lies in this. I lie to myself, though I don't know what about. Sometimes I wonder if I have made all these problems up in my head, though if that's true then I'm still not normal. I feel the void all the time though, and that is not a lie. It calls to me, whispering truths I cannot comprehend. I write this not with pride, bravado or brevity but just to explain the network I built to fund my habits. My headlong charge to push things as far as they would go would always cause this network to be unsustainable. How I kept the balls juggling till my mind collapsed first, I will never know.

It's official. I'm ostracised from my friends. Old Firm day, and I spent it with my two closest friends, one Catholic, one Protestant, not that it matters. They rest of the group now do not want to hang about with me. No one wants to take drugs round me in case they are caught with the smoking gun. I just want things to go back to normal. I don't want to change my whole circle of friends over my idiocy. Knowing I had to make my friends make this choice is gut wrenching. Years of being clean could make things better, or a blizzard of drugs on my behalf could make them see that they are not accomplices. I dunno which way to go.

My memory foam mattress has forgotten me, I fear my family will follow suit. My wife is so switched on to my schemes, now she is not pregnant, exhausted, and knows what to look for. I've taken to popping all my pills out of the packaging and keeping them in a sunglasses case, because she knows what any crinkling sound coming from me is. There is always a way to be sneakier. Always another layer of lies I can add.

I have come full circle, I think. I am back where I began, I can tell, with these scattered writings and broken thoughts. Each day is as slow as a week in the jail. I'm imprisoned in my own mind. Locked up with these evil thoughts with no way to vent them, because I am being denied drugs. My mum has put the word out on the street that no one is to deal to me. My scary Glaswegian pal has also sent the message, with dire consequences for anyone who disobeys him. Still, secrets within secrets. I have set up a PO box, and now I just get mail delivered there from Telegram then collect it at my leisure. There really is no way to stop me getting gear. The choice has to come from me, and as far as I am concerned, I can quit any time, as long as it's tomorrow, Coup d'état, world police and the evil we turn a blind eye to. Can we ever forgive ourselves for what we have done to each other? When I dwell on these thoughts, I am glad that in my heart I know I am not part of this problem. I have empathy for all races, creeds, colours and sexual orientations. The only evil I pass into the world is taken onto myself. I am the solitary victim. I know there is collateral, and I chastise myself for this. The only antidote to mental suffering is physical pain, after all, Marx said.

I also know I am full of contradictions.

At first, I wanted democratic shift then got disillusioned completely with politics when Scotland bottled it on voting to become an independent nation. The only nation in the history of the world to be so Fucking stupid. Then I wanted revolution, abolition of social inequality and the redistribution of wealth. Proper French Revolution, off with the heads of every monarch CEO and world leader in the land. As my mental health deteriorates, I just want anarch. Let the word burn. The skies could rip asunder, the oceans rise and society crumble.

We are turning into a dictatorship, and we have been taught to fear the witches, not those who burn them.

I'm dying to live. When I'm on drugs it's almost as if I live in a fantasy world. I get the skewed view that because I'm high, I have got one up on everyone else. Flawed opinion that drugs give me an advantage. I have something that they are missing out on. A superiority complex on top of a superiority complex. Layers and layers of madness and shite. Sometimes, but not often, I get a moment of clarity and a wave of disgust about how I feel hits me, and I scrabble back into my hole of ignorance and snobbery.

My email is icaruswings. I have had that since I was twelve. Why is it I was reading about Greek mythology at that age, and why was I drawn to the one story of a boy who flew too close to the sun? Why have I always wanted to crash and burn? Life is boring without a crisis.

I think too much. I dwell on things and turn an imagined slight in a conversation into a monster in my head. Then quiet it with drugs.

And who do I blame? Myself? Certainly not.

My partner? My parents? Evolution? God?

Whoever is to blame, if there is blame to be had, had no part in me taking the gift of fire from heaven and using it to burn down my house. My mind is on repeat. Same old stories, same old problems and same old thoughts. I am a broken record.

Into the Black

February

This may seem like a diary of a madman, and in some respects, it is. I started a diary of sorts the day after my overdose (death) in that tomb of a bathroom. This is what has developed into the scattered scribblings in interludes. The writing has been cathartic, and in reality, it is what has saved me. I felt at the time that I needed to get it all out and then I was free to die. As the voices receded, this urgency did as well. There is no doubt in my mind I was born with these problems. Bipolar, schizophrenia, BPD and addiction are all genetic. I stand firmly on the nature side in the nature versus nurture debate

I could not have been born into a more loving family. My poor, poor family. My dad's heart is in the right place and I love him so much for it. He has always been a strong father figure, I have just been a stronger tear away. I have amazing friends who have been there for me through every nightmare I endured, and the family I created for myself is a god-send (not that kind of god), yet I still turned into a raving monster addict. Loving my wife and fathering two sons are my proudest accomplishments and things I have always wanted but they are a double-edged sword. They gave the world a stick to beat me with.

Before I needed nothing, no one and feared only spiders. Now I need my family like a need air and I am terrified of losing them or any hurt befalling them. This puts a stick in my spokes and ribs on my quest of self-destruction.

137

I had the perfect nurturing environment, and my innate nature still clawed itself to the surface. My mind is still a work in progress; I feel as though I have just papered over the cracks. The fact that I can read something I wrote several months ago and still feel an affinity with it is worrying.

The ending is what I fear the most and what I am struggling against. Relapses are to be expected, but will it be a relapse where I finally let go, let the whispers on the wind take me? Take the final deep breath before the plunge. Only time will tell, and after all, it is better to burn out than to fade away.

What is addiction? It's never-ending escapism. An exile from pain. A hook in your heart. Looking back at some of my writing makes me see how deeply it had hold over me. It still does but now I see it as my enemy, not my ally.

I'm amazed at how my thinking has changed these past months. Not in the deeper thoughts that scream in my head that something is still missing in my life. But the thinking on the surface. I bought a four hundred quid iPad with my wages this month. The Martin of a few months ago would be furious at me, as that could have bought a q of cocaine. When I got my wages, I never counted them in pounds, only in grams.

I bought this iPad, as I am starting university again. I can't even remember applying. It was when I was staying with my parents, still high as a kite, managing to smuggle coke and pills past two diligent wardens. It wasn't their fault, they just don't understand the mind of an addict so can't understand the ways we keep ourselves alive. I can't remember applying, but I know why I did, because it's the same reason I'm fighting to stay clean now. I don't want to leave my boys.

As much as I do, I don't.

I took self-destruction as far as it could go, and it didn't work, so I grasped at a chance of self-improvement (*Fight Club* has a lot to answer for: I even named my son Tyler). I have even started playing football again. It's been over two years since I kicked a ball, and I didn't know how much I missed it till I was nearly passing out from lack of puff. Maybe I can make this.

Narcissistic. I am narcissistic to the point of no return. Another reason why I hate myself. Just let me sleep, an eternal sleep. Sleeping is an escape, as it is like being dead without hurting my family.

Sometimes I think Jesus loves me, but it's awkward, 'cos I only like him.

I have had a read of everything I have written, and fuck me, what a scattered mess my mind is. Three mental health diagnoses, god knows how many addictions and a filthy mouth to boot. I tried to stop swearing once, but I cunt.

I'm sitting in the place where it all ended. Or where it all began, really. Sitting in the downstairs bathroom where I took a trip downtown. I can't quite grasp who the person was that did the things in here. Who the fuck was I? I smoked so much crack in this room, shot up so much cocaine without anyone knowing. How the fuck did I get away with it? I would be sitting talking to someone in the living room, nip to the toilet, find a vein, then pop back out mid-conversation.

How is it I was so lost, but veins could always be found? Who was that person who did these things? I am utterly ashamed, but I have got to give myself some credit. I made an art out of being a junkie. Hiding in plain sight. Opaque and full of hate. I fucking loathe the person I was, but I can't help missing him. That hook is too deeply embedded for the longing to ever go to

139

sleep.

From the depths my pain and in its voices I drown. Pulled down to the lightness abyss. Abandon all hope, sea and be lost. I danced my death throes to the bed and let them fall like a leaf on the first crack of frost. In goes the needle, out comes the pain. I love you in the evening and in the morning rain.

I got to thinking of Russell the other day. I fucking miss him, man. One of my best mates who died suddenly, complications with a health condition, he just didn't wake up one morning.

He had the most energy and the brightest outlook on life. He was a DJ and called himself a local celebrity. We would go to gigs together, chase girls and take drugs. He was a laugh a minute, I fucking miss him and I want to join him. The urge to rebel is so strong in me, and I just feel I'm chained in a gilded cage. No options open to me in this world. Drugs seem to be the only rebellion left. Standing outside Russell'sone night, having a fag, he looked out over the lights of Inverness and said, "Look at my city, eh. This is my city."

He was right, and I miss him.

Looking back at my writing is horrifying to me now. Too see how much the drugs had twisted my mind, how they convinced me to lie to myself, bound by the threat of full consciousness. My beliefs have not changed but have been cemented by the memories from my overdose. I wasn't even self-aware, like a computer coded to follow a strict routine of wake, placate, sleep.

Keeping my nose clean in more ways than one is all I can do now for my family. Even the pain I still feel inside must be endured. It is the price I have to pay to keep my thoughts my own.

I have had to exorcise the old me. Pry him off with every ounce of free will I have. And now I have imposter syndrome in my own life. I don't know how to act, how to speak to people or even how to think, lest it sets me sauntering back down old paths.

I think I'm going to make it now, if only for my family's sake. I am determined to make this up to my wife, to spend my whole life making it up to her, for at the end of the day, this is a love story. A story of how her love pulled a madman back from the brink of insanity and death and made him part of his family again. How my love for her drives me every day to try and make up for the horrors I brought upon her, and how I just want to make her smile. How our combined love will raise our kids never to turn out like their father.

We are on holiday at my uncles in Spain, and my two sons are playing in the pool. My wife is bathed in sunlight and radiant as ever only shown up by my daughters beauty. She looks over at me curiously. Concerned.

"Marty, you okay? What you thinking about?"

I can't quite feel the sunlight on my skin yet, but I'm close.

"Nothing, hen, you know my head is full of pish and broken biscuits. All I'm really thinking about is you later with your legs at quarter to three."

"Shut up, Marty, the boys can hear."

"Ach, they can't tell the time. Anyway, I love you."

"I love you too."

She really is an angel.

No One Knows

March

It has been over a year since my overdose. Everything seems forgotten by everyone except me. I will never really heal. I don't think there is a cure for what is wrong with me. I am still sad, conflicted, angry, lost, and I still don't know why. Everything and nothing has changed. Well, my friends seem to think it has, and it's all water under the bridge is safe from drowning as I am offered a line at a party. Opportunity knocks, only it's the devil at the door and he brought all his toys. Who am I to refuse such a polite gesture? Here we go again.

It all seems a surreal dream. One big trip and I didn't stop falling till I hit the rocks at the bottom. I lost my way, and how I got back to where I am now is a miracle, or a testament to my will. I am leaning on the latter. Or a third option that I was dragged, kicking and screaming. Kidnapped from my dark cocoon of drugs and thrown into the cruel world by the scruff of my neck.

I feel like the answers I got were the ones I wanted, not the ones I needed. There is deeper shit in my past and in my head, but even my subconscious knows to gloss over it. A sub-conscience within. I don't even know who's calling the shots any more. I don't dare delve. Why poke the bear? Think I'll sit back and let the drugs run the show again.

April

Where is my mind?

The only fear I have acknowledged all my life, the only deep feeling I have not suppressed, is the fear of missing out. I have fed this fear, stoked it to a blaze. I fear that somewhere, someone is doing something that I am missing. That I need. There is a party I could be attending, a girl I could be fucking, just something that I am missing in my life. Anything to quell this urgency I have inside, this itch I can't scratch. What is it I am missing? A councillor told me that after thirty days off coke, your brain rewires itself. Healed and you can feel the sun on your face again. At the time I laughed in his face, and now I've made it past thirty-nine days, I want to call him a cunt. There is no sunshine on my face.

I don't feel the sunlight on my skin at all any more. I sit ten feet back from my eyes. Lights and sounds flicker in but they can't fill this cavern. It is cold and oppressive and I am not alone.

I told my psychiatrist had a dream I was attacked by a monster last night. It was my addiction and was all claws and a ravenous maw and it was slashing its claws down my arms. When I woke up it's marks were still there, my faded tram lines.

I feel I have a twisted ouroboros in my gut. The call of the void makes me take drugs to escape it and the drugs make me long for escape even more. A perpetual, vicious cycle, until the serpent chokes on its own tail. I am happy living my shallow and insignificant life. You can drown in a deep and meaningful one.

Some shite I have told my psychiatrist. He has had to get a psychiatrist of his own now. Thank God for the Hippocratic oath.

My mind is fractured and all I think about is shooting up. All the colours have faded from the world and the joy sucked out without cocaine in my veins. I can't get no sleep. I toss and turn on a bed of nails, dreaming about needles.

May

Josh killed himself yesterday. He told me he was going to do it and I couldn't save him. Came to see me after not going into work and he was already out his face on trams. 1300 mg deep. He has the constitution of a rhino. It was the end of the month and we were both skint, no goblins in sight. He came to see me because he knew I would give him no patronising answers. No "it's going to be okay, pal. Everything will get better" from me. I know the blackness, the call of the void. I couldn't tell him it would get better because I don't know if it will for me either. We are both fighting the same monster. All I could give him was reasons not to do it. Hold on for your sons, for his mum. He said he had held on for twenty years for his sons, he was exhausted and he had made peace with leaving his mum. He wanted to be at peace like another friend from SPL who had recently killed himself. Josh had threatened suicide before and we both have talked about it so many times I have lost count but this time seemed different. He had been up all-night fighting with his bird. I told him to come into mine for a sleep but he wouldn't. He promised me, he would go home to his mum's for a sleep and call me when he woke. I took his remaining two strips of trams off him and let him go. He did go home for a bit then told his mum he was away for fags. I got out the shower to a frantic phone call from his mum. Told her to phone the police but when I looked at my messages, I knew he had done it. He message me saying goodbye, that I was a good man and a true friend. My world dropped, I knew he was dead there and then and those were the last words I would ever get from him. This has broken me man. He told me we were Thelma and Louise but he drove off the cliff without me. Where's the needle.

The highlands has the second highest suicide rate in Scotland. Slightly behind Dundee but still nearly twice the average of the rest of Scotland. Scotland has the highest rate in the UK and the highlands with 23.5 suicides per 100k people would make it in the top ten countries with the worst suicide rate in the world.

Why is the picturesque highlands of Scotland suffering from a suicide pandemic of young men? We live in a beautiful part of the world, a first world country that does not have a war on its shores and in fact has never been conquered. We have a free health service, job opportunities and no tyrant ruling over us. We have a high quality of life so why are we taking our own?

Only behind acts of god, suicide is the number one killer for males under forty-five. Why? How do we become so depressed that we make the final choice? If god doesn't strike us down in a fatal accident, we choose to do his job for him and wash down a tub of sleeping tablets with a bottle of vodka. We have lost our place in this world. Hunter gatherers forced to flip a switch or push a button to earn minimum wage. All the while being bombarded with Facebook ads for holidays and clothes, we will never be able to enjoy. Offered a linear path through life, chained to our phone in our gilded cage. Depression seeps in and we turn down it's volume with drink and drugs. These are plasters on a tumour. What are health services to do when it is society that causes the sickness? Talking to a psychiatrist can only go so far, I know. A mundane preordained narrative to our lives, add to that debt, hopelessness and despair. All the pretty hills in the world ain't gonna stop you climbing in the bath with the toaster. I have no answers, I'm still crying out for one. Only my wife and kids keep me tethered to this world. Other people are not so lucky and they cut their own cord to drift off into oblivion. I have an indescribable feeling of emptiness, something missing, being born out of place and out of time. No matter how pretty my chains are, I'm still a slave. I fight to stay alive in my own head every day.

Fuck knows if this is how the suicide statistics felt or if anyone else is afflicted by the same thoughts as me now.

Suicide is contagious. Weighed down by the weight of the world, a young man hears about a man in similar circumstances as him that has taken his own life. And so, a seed is planted. It sprouts, takes root and grows tendrils into every crevice of your subconscious. Life remains tough as only life can and now the only answer you can think of is the one screamed at you by this jungle of poison ivy inside your mind. What was once a sad story you never thought would apply to yourself has now infested every manner of your thinking. You hang yourself on your thoughts then it is your suicide that is gossiped about your town. A sad young man hears the tale. And so on and so forth.

Sic Transit Gloria Mundi

There was nothing special about today, no trigger for relapse that no doubt people will analyse. I don't even think it has anything to do with my manic depression. The voices are there, yes, but that's still not why. The pull of the drugs is too strong; the hook's in too deep. As with most things in my life, there was no thought process, just pure, innate intuition of what I needed. Since my death, I had been fighting every day, forcing myself to actually make decisions, because when I do, I make the correct ones.

There was no decision made; instinct just took over. Coke bought, chemist visited and needles picked up (god bless the NHS). Then bathroom door locked. My wife was away for the weekend with the kids, so I had the time to myself. And that was about as much as they factored into the equation. I was just like Bilbo: I went out of the door and didn't keep my feet. Off I trot on a narcotic adventure.

As you can see, I have not learned my lesson. I prepare the shot of cocaine with a surgeon's precision and a lover's touch. I can feel a crescendo building in me. I have loaded it with coke. I don't know if it will kill me, and I don't care. I have let go. I am a boat adrift in a sea of voices again.

I push down on the syringe. Deep exhale. The music fades away and the party stops. The voices change tone and volume. I can hear Rand laughing now, his smug, gleeful laugh booming in my ears. My face smacks the tiles on the bathroom floor again. It was not a tabula rasa after all.

There is no rebirth this time, no redemption. The stage is set, and no one shouts "Encore". We all die alone, which is fine with me. Death is always waiting in the wings, biding it's time, waiting to pluck you from your insignificant life and soar into the great beyond.

We are shadows on the wall and when we meld with the unknown, the reality that casts the shadows will be revealed.

Finally, the audience in my head is silent.